John Mossman

THE GREAT CENTURIES OF PAINTING

COLLECTION PLANNED AND DIRECTED BY

ALBERT SKIRA

THE GREAT CENTURIES OF PAINTING

THE SEVENTEENTH CENTURY

THE NEW DEVELOPMENTS IN ART FROM

CARAVAGGIO TO VERMEER

TEXT BY JACQUES DUPONT AND FRANÇOIS MATHEY

Translated by S. J. C. Harrison

SKIRA

GENEVA PARIS NEW YORK

The colorplate of the title page:
St Sebastian mourned by St Irene (Georges de La Tour)

ITALY · FRANCE
SPAIN · FLANDERS · HOLLAND

CARAVAGGIO · SARACENI · TER BRUGGHEN

RIBERA · LA TOUR · VELAZQUEZ

LE NAIN · CHAMPAIGNE · FRANS HALS · REMBRANDT

RUBENS · VAN DYCK · POUSSIN

CLAUDE · BASCHENIS · BAUGIN · ZURBARAN

VAN STREECK · SEGHERS

VERMEER · RUISDAEL · HOBBEMA

THERE are sound reasons for the great contemporary interest in the XVIIth century; for the artists of that century re-stated and found new solutions to all the problems of creative art. The glorious age of the Renaissance had ended, a period of decadence had set in, and it was clear to the forward-looking spirits of the period that an entirely fresh start was called for. Once again they had to scrutinize the real world around them, master the forms of nature, discover for themselves expressive rhythms, the laws of a constructive handling of sensory data and the organization of Space. The amazing thing is that all these ends were achieved, not in the course of a slow evolution extending over centuries, but almost simultaneously, within a few years, and in quite different countries. Hence that impression the century gives us of an immense profusion, an abundance of creative genius that seems indeed unique, as compared with earlier or subsequent periods, when the world of art was dominated by a single school, whether Italian, Flemish or French. But in the XVIIth century, throughout Western Europe—in Italy, in Spain, in France and in the Low Countries—there were parallel developments and discoveries, implementing and supplementing each other.

Many of these discoveries had a tectonic quality of the highest order; they 'built up' new worlds of visual experience. Our modern predilection for such painters as Caravaggio, Velazquez and Vermeer is due to the solutions they offered for the age-old problems of the artist: of expression, the matière, and composition. And our program here is not so much to give an historical survey as to indicate what, in this vast heritage, seems to us most worthy of attention.

At the beginning of the present century interest centered on the Carracci, Guido Reni, Murillo, Le Sueur, Lebrun and the Dutch 'Little Masters,' whose noble sentiments or quaintness appealed to the taste prevailing in a wealthy bourgeoisie. The sudden promotion to the front rank of Caravaggio and his school and the discovery of the Le Nains and Georges de La Tour are not due to chance or a mere change of fashion. The achievements of Impressionism, of Cubism with its penchant for abstraction—the sacrifice of the subject to the object—and all the discoveries of modern art have helped us to a better under-standing of the great endeavors of the past. But our modern art, when it deliber-ately confines itself to problems of composition or technique, and ventures on the study of man only with extreme circumspection, almost apologetically, usually leaves us with a vague impression that something important has been left out. Thus we tend to hail as nothing short of miraculous the art of a provincial *painter like La Tour : an art which, if somewhat cursory, is yet complete, in the sense that, while finding for himself solutions of essentially pictorial problems much like ours, he always gave thought to the psychology of his model, however commonplace.*

Still it must be granted that if we do not accord equal admiration to Poussin and Lebrun (as would have been done a century ago), it is because the skillful composition of the former appeals to our present taste for geometry and form, whereas the mere technical proficiency of Lebrun leaves us cold. And if nowadays we can better appreciate Caravaggio's realism and Rubens' Baroque luxuriance, it well may be that Claudel's Le Soulier de Satin *has shaped our taste accordingly. For our fathers Rembrandt was the greatest of all, because his gravity impressed them; for us too he remains the greatest of his age, and not for purely aesthetic reasons but because he is the only artist who solved that eternal, ever urgent, problem of doubt and faith.*

The reason why our generation, inured—though we are loath to admit it— to the absence of any authentically human element in art, harks back with such enthusiasm to the XVIIth century, is doubtless because that century faced up to the plastic problems which hold our interest today, but without shutting its eyes to the spiritual and human mission of all great art.

PAINTING IN THE SEVENTEENTH CENTURY

WHEN we think of XVIIth-century painting, we conjure up an image of billowing drapery in a church cupola where angels flutter around the ecstatic figure of a martyr saint ; or we conjure up sedate still lifes of carefully arranged flowers and fruits, earnest faces telling of devout souls, children carrying tapers, bonneted housewives and pictures of watery countries with far horizons lit up only by the brief smile of a sail. Painting was at the same time bombastic, serene, mythological, homely, aristocratic and bourgeois. Yet in spite of the great variety of schools, the XVIIth century has one unifying feature. This is the persistence of the religious spirit throughout Europe : clerical in the spheres of Hapsburg influence ; Jansenist or Gallican, but personal, in France ; individualistic in the Reformation countries. Artistic expression varies with the social setting, temperament and generation. The diverse, often contradictory, nature of the pictorial methods adopted tends to make us forget that all aspire to be solutions of the same enigma, the great problem set by the men of the Renaissance— that of human destiny.

Lack of ballast in the idealism of the Renaissance, leading to the Mannerists in Rome and the School of Fontainebleau in France, soon called for a return to a more objective handling of reality. In spite of its eclecticism, its haste to annex whatever served its turn in the work of the three giants—Leonardo, Raphael and Michelangelo— the academicism of the Carracci was also a move against anarchy in the types of subjects chosen and against the excessive license taken by painters in interpreting the themes assigned them. According to his individual genius each reacted in his own way. The painter more sensitive to line, by applying himself to the problem of exact composition ; the painter guided mainly by his instinct, by trying to render the effects of light. It was the eternal dispute between the moderns and the classicists which obtained as well between Caravaggio and the Carracci as between the followers of Rubens and those of Poussin. The same problem also occupied the later Baroque painters following Rubens, who tried with varying success to combine both tendencies.

The Council of Trent drew up an official iconography, which was tantamount to a new aesthetic and even a new code of ethics. This was done in order to halt the fanciful interpretations, on almost surrealist lines, of the sacred narrative authoritatively recorded in the Vulgate. This also entailed the suppression of everything superfluous or foreign to the Bible story. For these painters, who were often members of the Third Order, as at the Academy of Saint Luke, were auxiliaries to the theologians and shared in their vocation of teaching and glorifying the Church. On the one hand were the public preachers—meaning the decorators following the school of the Carracci (what mattered the thought if the gesture were sublime ?) ; on the other, prayer and meditation : represented by the personal, instinctive art of Caravaggio, falling so well in line with the spiritual exercises of Loyola.

The great originality of Caravaggio lay in his use of chiaroscuro. He preferred suggestion to direct statement. One might say that this method corresponds to the setting of a Shakespearian tragedy, where every secondary color is toned down to set off the hero.

To be sure, others before him amongst the Milanese had exploited the potentialities of light and shadow; but, with Caravaggio, chiaroscuro became a system embraced by all Europe, with each painter modifying it to fit his particular talent. Before him, light had been no more than a source of pleasure and a test of skill. But as used by Caravaggio, light became the essence of the drama, sometimes forcing the actors back into a narrow strip of shadow ; or again, bringing them into a brilliant foreground, stressing the impassioned dialogue. Shadow and light were used quite arbitrarily ; but dramatic illusion was achieved, the action leapt across the footlights to grip a public of believers.

Rubens was another champion of the Faith ; he learned his lessons of Mannerism and Academicism in Rome, and his innate lyricism remolded them into a triumphant hymn of joy.

Meanwhile in France religious grandiloquence was not in vogue. Bossuet's eloquence was a literary form confined to the court. The Jansenists were wary of pompousness and the Vatican's outer show of piety ; it shocked their notion of free will and their iron belief in private worship. Caravaggio's strong, compelling contrasts of light and shade, emphasizing essentials and disregarding incidentals, were not congenial to the French way of thinking. The French mind demanded discretion and enlightened modesty. It ascribed equal importance to the essentials and the non-essentials. True, in France they continued to paint church altarpieces in the prevailing manner, but there was no religious conviction behind it. It was in the still life, the interior, the 'Vanitas,' and on the faces of the Jansenists that the spirit of the Church incarnate was made manifest.

A sense of man's redemption permeates the paintings of the Flemish Reformation countries. Rembrandt and Vermeer fashioned this spirit into intimate scenes which voiced the trustful fervor of the Pater Noster.

And at the time when Gallicans and Protestants were combating the militant art of Rome, the work of Poussin saw the day. Here was a man deaf to the religious tumult of his time. His interests were purely pictorial ; he located a picture within three unities like those of tragedy : space, reason and geometry. Because his genius was too exacting and he himself too independent, he had no followers. Hence his art strikes us as an isolated phenomenon ; yet none the less it changed the whole basis of painting. In his hands, art became an end in itself, and its function supremely aristocratic. By the end of the century, painting, which had started off by seeking to express the best in man, had completely lost touch with its mission and, only too ready to accept servitude, came to render homage only to the king.

It was in the Low Countries, haven of all imperiled freedoms, that painting remained most closely in touch with life. It illustrated the rude independence of that country, its pride and natural kindliness. Painters sought their subjects in the Flemish countryside, patiently ploughed by thrifty peasants who regarded comfortable circumstances as the condition of happiness, and man as being sufficient unto himself. And going beyond their conscious purpose, they summed up, if in a minor key, all that Western humanism stood for.

There was nothing abstract about this Western humanism. Rather, it was a vigorous reality which shaped all XVIIth-century Europe. Indeed it is this humanism which makes the Europe of that time, seen in the perspective of three hundred years, strike us as a united whole, an international republic. True, there was a diversity of governments and religious tenets, but all the States professed similar principles as to human rights, unknown in countries not directly shaped by Christian teachings. "It is because of these principles," said Voltaire with just pride as a good European, "that the nations of Europe do not take their prisoners into slavery, that they respect the ambassadors of the enemy ... and above all that they co-operate in the prudent policy of a balance of power between themselves." But this calm, which characterized the XVIIth-century mind as regards its art and politics, took many years in coming.

When Henry IV was assassinated in 1610, the forces of anarchy which had been kept down by him, but not destroyed, rose to the surface. And it took nearly half a century for Richelieu and Mazarin to quell them. Moreover, the religious peace, though now restored, was but precariously maintained.

At the end of the XVIth century and during the first half of the XVIIth, all the governments of Europe had to face what was nothing short of a widespread epidemic of unrest. Thus the Fronde was not a purely French but a European symptom. The great discoveries and the intellectual ferment, due to the Renaissance, had disturbed all the social orders of Europe, to the point of completely changing their aspect. They were conscious of their limitations and strove to thrust them back, and they cast about for new means of expression to meet their predicament. As against this, the forces of conservatism mustered their strength, while the central governments tended to enlarge their authority, and the aristocracy defended privileges they could no longer justify. Manuals of history make the modern age start in 1610, though there is no denying that the whole first half of the century was darkened by wars and the last upheavals of a world struggling to regain its balance. The Treaty of Westphalia in 1648 consecrated the liquidation of a past which had become meaningless, and it laid the foundations of contemporary Europe.

Spain lost much influence. She preferred the European dream of building up a precarious Holy Empire, to developing her conquests in the new world. Undoubtedly her decline was less obvious to her contemporaries than to us today. But the Treaty of Westphalia, the Peace of the Pyrenees and the War of Devolution were fatal wounds. To be sure, the Spain of Philip IV was still the Spain of Lope de Vega, of Calderon and Velazquez ; and the great victory of Spinola at Breda proved that her power was still very real. And no doubt the Spain of Charles II and Murillo retained that pomp and ceremony which dazzled Saint-Simon. She ruled over Belgium, Italy and the largest colonial empire in the world ; at the Vatican her influence was still preponderant. Though she no longer dominated Europe, all Europe was obsessed by her, and she still was the focal point of European politics. But her power was waning. Not content with winning their independence from Spain, the Dutch held up Spanish ships on the high seas and seized her most profitable markets in the Indian Archipelago and the Americas.

The younger branch of the Austrian Hapsburgs had ceased to be a danger. They were in a dilemma between the immediate need of conciliating their Protestant subjects with their own hereditary Catholicism. Their great dream of unifying Europe was ending. After 1648, sure of preserving their independence and self-determination, the nations of Europe were striking out for themselves. Domestic differences were by way of being appeased. The Protestants regained their freedom, while Catholicism staked all on the Counter-Reformation—and won. Though hampered by religious dissensions, the human spirit boldly moved forward again, and man was regaining confidence in himself.

The political outlook of Europe had never been so propitious. The financial organization of Holland, the most powerful in Europe and the envy of Colbert, was capable of supporting the huge East and West Indian Companies, which occupied Java and Malacca, discovered Australia and Tasmania and founded New Amsterdam—New York to be—on the Hudson. Holland was glutted with riches wrested, as was her mainland, from the sea. Tulips and hyacinths decked gardens, and piles of precious stones were stored in the captains' cabins in her ships.

Seen in history's perspective, the France of Richelieu and Mazarin is found to have possessed a latent power which did not come to light until the autocratic reign of Louis XIV. The marvelous stability that France enjoyed gave her the lead and enabled her to set the tone of Europe. Thus, confident in her future, she built not for the moment but for coming generations. The miracle of the XVIIth century lay precisely in this beneficent stability which Europe had never yet enjoyed. Louis XIV reigned until 1715. Leopold the Great reigned 47 years, Vittorio Amedeo 57, and Charles Emmanuel of Savoy from 1648 to 1675. William of Orange, elected Stadtholder in 1672, died in 1702, while in Spain Philip IV and Charles II, contrary to expectation, held the reins of power from 1620 to 1702. Europe accepted its multiplicity and did not trouble again about its equilibrium. The ambitions of governments were limited. Strategy and tactics were adjusted to the aims enjoined on them by politics. War, too, was treated 'classically,' and resorted to only for questions of succession and frontiers. Ambitious leaders no longer thought that victories brought any great change to the welfare of a nation, or that, if they entailed heavy sacrifices, they were 'paying propositions.'

This improvement in the European situation was widespread. But in this general well-being, it was France that chiefly profited. Yet her power and glory did not impair those of other nations ; the 'century' of Louis XIV did not eclipse the 'golden century' in Holland, nor should it obscure the achievements of Italy, Spain or England—as we shall see in this panoramic view of European painting.

1

PLAYS OF LIGHT
FORMS IN MOVEMENT
RENDERINGS OF VOLUME

CARAVAGGIO
GEORGES DE LA TOUR

AFTER *the passing of the Renaissance art was at the cross-roads. If the artist was to break with the tedious conventionality which had set in, the consequence of a protracted cult of 'the beautiful,' two ways lay open. Either he could add a psychological content to the picture by making it express his personal response to the thing seen; or he could hark back to essentials, things-as-they-are. In the first case it was needful to impart movement, the token of emotion, to the forms. Caravaggio, however, did not (as Rubens was to do) attempt to render continuous movement; he fixed on the momentary—the 'snap-shot.' The scene is shown up in a flash, each gesture is cut short midway, as though the person making it had suddenly been turned to stone. Thus the elements of visual experience acquired a somewhat theatrical, strongly expressive, style—a procedure that pointed the way to modern Expressionism.*

Georges de La Tour illustrates the other method : the quest of form-in-itself—as it exists, unconditioned by the artist's personal responses, in the natural world. La Tour expresses this conquest of his intuition by a simplification of volumes, by the exclusion of all accidental or artificial elements, and the abandonment of all idea of transformation. Static and independent, these volumes are built up objectively in terms of their own requirements—a method resembling that subsequently followed by the Cubists.

ROME AND CARAVAGGIO

After being sacked by the imperial troops in the early years of the XVIth century, there seemed left of Rome, as Pope Clement VII put it, "no more than a ragged corpse." Yet life went on and the end of the century saw a new era of Roman prosperity, sustained by an ever more vigorous Papacy whose voice of authority rang out with an effect unknown since the XIIIth century. As Philip II ruled his empire from the Escorial, so Gregory XIII and Sixtus V made the Vatican the heart and center of Christendom, whose spiritual hegemony was to spread overseas as far as Japan and the New World. The centralization of ecclesiastical administration in Rome, the influx of gold from the Indies and the Americas, the creation of the 'congregations,' the need that was felt both by governments and the numerous religious Orders—Capuchins, Barnabites, Ursulines, Theatines and the like—to be represented at the Holy See, involved the building of new palaces, convents and churches. The Rome we know today was beginning to take form. However, though the Church was resolved to exercise the greatest firmness in foreign policy, she showed, faithful to her old tradition, benevolent liberalism as to art. And so vast were the projects undertaken that artists poured in from all the Catholic countries of Europe. "To Rome, more than to any other place, the painters tend to come, for hers are the greatest schools of painting," writes Van Mander. "Art is the national sport." Rome drew all talent to her and the Church courted the artist as the best exponent of her power and interpreter of her doctrines. With his Church of Gesù, Vignola fixed the style of a new collective spirituality, which found its expression in the worldwide communion of believers and was spread everywhere by Jesuit missions. Vignola published his *Rule of the Five Orders* and Palladio his *Treatise on Architecture*, and these became the architects' handbooks. At work in this stimulating climate were Baroccio, a late follower of Correggio, the Mannerist group, Vasari, Taddeo and Federigo Zuccheri, Caravaggio, and the Carracci (who painted the ceilings in the Farnese Gallery). All were welcomed with equal favor and enjoyed the same undiscriminating admiration, often from the very same patrons. For there was no question—as is often thought today—of their being ranged in opposing schools or fanatically pitted against each other. That artistic *milieu* of XVIIth-century Rome, where Flemings rubbed shoulders with Neapolitans, Frenchmen with Spaniards, Bolognese with Germans, Lorrainese with Venetians, must have been very much like the Montparnasse of 1920-1925.

We should be wrong, however, to speak of any specifically Roman School, for the Carracci brought their aesthetic with them from Bologna, while Callot came from Nancy with his Lorrainese Expressionism, and Caravaggio from Milan. All the painters of that day whom we now tend to group in sharply demarcated 'schools' were in reality continually taking a leaf from each other's books, so to speak, and exchanging the technical recipes of often distant studios where they had learnt the *métier*. And if no Roman School can properly be spoken of, despite the presence of a central power whose very essence was unity, how much less are we justified in speaking of an Italian School, considering the vast differences between the styles of painting at Venice, Bologna and Naples! There was no more an Italian School than a French or Spanish. These categories served the turn of historians afterwards, but they had no real existence at the time. Only this much can we say : like causes produced like effects, differentiated only by the genius of the individual. The Edicts of the Council of Trent, on the one hand, and the reactions in various countries to mannerist painting, on the other, brought forth Caravaggio in Italy, Velazquez in Spain, and La Tour and the Le Nains in France. Thanks to his spectacular qualities, Caravaggio has come to be looked on by art critics as the Master of all the other realists and the name 'Caravaggism,' actually that of a brief local outgrowth, has tended to fix itself to similar contemporary phases of European art. To deny obvious influences in this painting would be to go to another extreme, but neither must we overstress them to the point of decrying the innate genius of the painters of reality. We now grant Caravaggio and his followers a large place in our esteem (their own age thought less highly of them), because their work has remarkable affinities with the trends of our modern art. The last century would have treated Caravaggio's art as a side-issue, and assigned Guido Reni and Guercino the leading roles in XVIIth-century painting at Rome.

When Michelangelo Merisi, son of a bricklayer's hand employed in the Lombard town of Caravaggio, came in 1588 to Rome, a raw youth, ready to turn his hand to anything, he was already bent on making his career in art. At Milan he had nothing more to learn from Peterzano, for he had quickly come to the end of that teacher's store of knowledge, and absorbed the lessons of the Bergamo and Brescia painters: Lotto, Moroni, Savoldo and the Morettos. There was work to be had in Rome, and he felt sure of making good. He found employment with a Roman painter, Il Cavaliere d'Arpino, for whom he did many of his early works, content for the moment to play a small part and bide his time. Looking about him, he found the work of other painters false and sterile, a far cry from his own ideal : "To paint natural things well and correctly." He was hard-working, self-willed, warm-hearted, and very soon his high spirits attracted the notice of his patron's friends. Monsignor Petriani was the first to take an interest in him and offered him hospitality. It is a remarkable feature of Caravaggio's brief but eventful career that no matter how great the trials to which he put the patience and kindness of his patrons, their faith in him never wavered. And they knew their man. How indeed could so many high dignitaries of the Church, such men as Cardinals Del Monte, Sennezio, Gonzaga and Scipione Borghese, have been mistaken as to the merits of their protégé ? Actually all we know about him is the reputation foisted on him by his rivals, Bellori, Mancini and Baglione, who represent him as a swashbuckling type in the manner of Cellini, a murderer and an outlaw, *fantastico e bestiale*. The trick is an old one : blacken a man's character the better to discredit his work. And we may feel sure that as against the cheap religiosity of Zuccaro, and even of the Carracci, Caravaggio's uncompromising realism, as hard-hitting as Rouault's today, could but shock the pious conformity of the clergy and all respectable citizens of Rome.

The future belongs to those who love life, and Caravaggio loved it passionately. This was when Bacchus was his favorite subject ; always he depicted the same budding youth, with a dreamy, love-smitten expression on a full, sensual face, and cheeks with the downy bloom of the ripe fruit we find in his still lifes. Caravaggio could on occasion yield to this pagan glorification of youth—of youth that passes all too soon—but his true bent was different. Despite his keen enthusiasm for life under its every aspect, he was by nature simple, country-bred, God-fearing ; and probably his father confessor

37 yrs of life,

CARAVAGGIO (1573-1610). THE FORTUNE-TELLER, CA. 1590. (39½×51½″) LOUVRE, PARIS.

Dutch and Flemish 'petits maîtres' had much fondness for depicting gamblers, sharpers and the like ; here Caravaggio has used a similar theme, that of the Fortune-teller, and made of it an excellent 'set piece.' Very probably this scene is an allegory or a modernized version of a stock subject of traditional iconography, like 'The Prodigal Son' and 'The Sorceress.'

had made him realize the futility of such lawless loves. Thus when he paints the Magdalen at prayer—a pretext with his fellow painters for ingenious displays of semi-nudity—Caravaggio takes care to veil with sumptuous garments the comely body of the sinner, and all he seeks to express is his fraternal pity for a poor girl who might have come like him from his birthplace, Caravaggio, and has somehow gone astray in this corrupt city of Rome, but, unlike him, failed to come to terms with life.

SINCERE

The problems of the human situation are as diverse as the minds of man; of Caravaggio it can be said that, all his lapses notwithstanding, he was a man of good will.

Such was his respect for truth that Caravaggio never dreamt of expressing nature otherwise than she is. He was the opposite of an artist—in other words, he was a painter. And as such, he had to express forcibly what he felt, whereas 'artists' can only refine on what they see. He was aware of the dramatic element latent in men's lives and the illusions that encompass them. Drama and illusion—shadow and light—these are the two directives of his art.

It was in a form of realist 'luminism' that Caravaggio found the perfect expression of his genius—so much so that we instinctively associate this with his name. He did not, however, invent this technique. The Milanese masters under whom he studied, the Peterzanos and the Campi, had formed his taste for seeing things as they nakedly are, with an objectivity heightened by a play of luminous effects. And before his time, as he well knew, Correggio and the Bassanos had struck out in this direction. Annibale Carracci himself, though he has been thrust into the background now that Caravaggio has come into his own, was not far from the latter's naturalistic approach when he painted his *Bean Eater*. Actually, however, it is in Titian and Tintoretto that we may find the true masters of the painters we call "Tenebrosi," for the restlessness we associate with their art is much more in the mood of the Renaissance than in that of the Counter-Reformation.

A level-headed man, untouched by the academicism of his day, Caravaggio followed in the footsteps of his father, a Lombard stonemason. Like an architect, he built up his pictures with light and shade, with plena and vacua. He painted what he saw because it never occurred to him to deal in sublimations, because houses are not built of dreams and allegories. Because everyday life and people provide the most fascinating models if only one can wrest their secrets from them. Who knows what those secrets really are? They themselves do not know—so readily do we go astray when we try to understand ourselves. A man's truth is the idea he has of himself. "Reality" is not his natural self, it is the outer layer, hiding the smoldering drama beneath the surface. Appearances may mislead, and the shrewd countryman that Caravaggio was remains a realist even when he idealizes his figures. When he paints a Bacchus he obviously idealizes, giving him conventional beauty of form, almost abstract in treatment, with the usual folds of drapery stylized in the best academic manner. Yet a real person is there, perhaps the good-looking shopkeeper round the corner— or his wife.

CARAVAGGIO (1573-1610). FRUIT AND FOLIAGE, ?1590. (18×25″) AMBROSIANA, MILAN.

This still life comes from the collection of Cardinal Fr. Borromeo ; treated with 'illusionist realism,' it illustrates the 'light manner' of Caravaggio's early phase (about 1596). The asymmetrical composition can be accounted for only if we assume this to be a fragment of some big picture (now lost) which the painter re-made ; this is suggested by the fact that the original background has obviously been painted over. Caravaggio is known to have been employed by the Cavaliere d'Arpino who used him for painting in the settings of his own compositions. Caravaggio usually included an isolated still life, treated as a bravura piece, in his portrayals of Bacchus, and in other paintings of his first phase.

After 1590, however, as if some unpleasant incident had abruptly cut short his enthusiasm, a change came ; Caravaggio was no longer satisfied with mere physical beauty. All that interests him now is the form of shadows falling on bodies, as if to

CARAVAGGIO (1573-1610). THE VOCATION OF ST MATTHEW, CA. 1593. (129×137″)
CHURCH OF SAN LUIGI DEI FRANCESI, ROME.

This picture is one of a sequence dealing with St Matthew's life which Caravaggio painted for the Contarelli Chapel in the Church of S. Luigi dei Francesi ; it included *The Vocation of St Matthew, The Martyrdom of St Matthew* and *St Matthew and the Angel* (a first version of which was in the Berlin Museum, where it was destroyed in 1945). This *Vocation* was the first official order Caravaggio was given for a church. The commission was obtained for him by Virgilio Crescenzi, executor of the will of Cardinal Matteo Cointrel, and under the patronage of Cardinal Del Monte. It is a typical example of veil in darkness the drama going on within, or to hint at it in sudden gleams of light. His distribution of light and shade followed a trend which, while its basic principles remained the same, became more and more accentuated, and was directly related to the vicissitudes of his life. After the period of clean-cut, limpid light, which produced the Bacchus pictures and still lifes realistically treated, he forsook worldly subjects and turned exclusively to religious themes. These he plunged into atmospheres of ever-increasing gloom from which the figures stand out like statues carved by a pitiless light that grips them, holds them prisoner. With the *St Matthew* in San Luigi dei Francesi at Rome, he set the style he kept to the end, and whose tragic possibilities, both in theme and treatment, he exploited to the utmost in his later work.

It would be interesting to know whether some sudden inspiration came to Caravaggio at this time, for he now succeeded in breathing new life and immediacy into his subjects, while locating them in contemporary settings as XVth-century painters had done. Such is the dramatic intensity of these works that we feel he pictures himself as personally taking part in them. In that dimly-lit gambling den (of *The Vocation of St Matthew*), is it not Caravaggio himself to whom Christ's finger points, and who alone is stricken with remorse ? All the poetry of his art is present in that single ray of light coming from an unseen window and slanting across the dingy wall. A weak light, arbitrary perhaps, but far from artificial, for its suggestive power is great, hinting as it does at an airless, two-dimensional world, a prison-house whence there is no escaping for these men marked with life's scars and bound to their vocations. Like Manet's, this realism is untainted by vulgarity. Yet small minds took offense at it ; the shower of abuse his *St Matthew* brought down on the painter's head is evidence of the scandal this art provoked. These outbursts are not, however, to be charged up to the Church, but only to the bigots. Once calm returned and the picture had been withdrawn from the Church of San Luigi dei Francesi, for which he had commissioned it, Cardinal del Monte, unperturbed, went on ordering new works from Caravaggio. Apart from a few great connoisseurs like the Marquis Giustiniani and the Barbarini, his most loyal patrons were Cardinals of the Roman Curia, and when the future Pope, Urban VIII, wanted his portrait made, it was to Caravaggio that he applied. Though still anathema to the many, realist painting could not but appeal to the forthright spirit of the church dignitaries who led the Counter-Reformation. They were in sympathy with the new art and sponsored its rise.

Caravaggio truckled to none. He was as deeply conscious of his vocation, as was St Paul, whose *Conversion*, commissioned by Tiberio Serezi for the Church of Santa Maria del Popolo, was refused, but later bought by Cardinal Sennezio. With his face in the foreground of the picture, St Paul is lying on his back, thunderstruck by the voice from heaven, blinded by the inrush of divine grace, literally God-possessed. Standing by, the passive tool of fate, his horse looms large, a majestic presence. The

Caravaggio's handling of such subjects. The incident is 'caught' at its most dramatic moment: "Follow me," Christ has said, and a peremptory gesture of the pointing, summoning hand implements the divine command. Here lighting is everything, a completely arbitrary lighting which abruptly shatters the surrounding darkness, arresting every movement, and enforcing on St Matthew the tremendous import of the Call.

whole scene is plunged in darkness ; a shaft of eerie light, coming from nowhere, hovers on the horse's flanks, pierces the eyes of St Paul and illuminates his arms, outstretched as in a crucifixion. The scene is more impressive than the reality which it images. Actually this dramatic incident took place at noon in the open desert on the road to Damascus. By doing away with the factors of time and place, Caravaggio lifted the event on to the plane of the transcendent. Then as now, the public expected the story to be told as they knew it ; lacking that familiar context and thrown back on their imagination, his contemporaries could see in the picture no more than a clumsy rider unlucky enough to slip off his horse at the turn of a dark alley, sprawling on the ground.

His *Death of the Virgin* caused no less offense, and the picture was refused by the friars of Santa Maria della Scala. Yet, soon afterwards, Cardinal Borghese bought three of his works, a *St John the Baptist*, a *St Jerome* and a *David*.

Caravaggio overstepped the limits laid down by the conventions of his age, and such iconographical conventions, sanctioned and imposed as they are by immemorial tradition, are apt to be as strict as primitive taboos. The masses are attached to them and woe to their transgressor ! In Caravaggio's *Death of the Virgin* we see a poor corpse brought from the morgue, her legs swollen, her face already bearing the tokens of decay. To be sure, the simple piety of the Middle Ages had not shrunk from a realistic treatment

of the Virgin, but never had it gone to such lengths as this in deliberately bringing the divine Mother of God down to so human a plane. We cannot question the sincerity and devoutness of Caravaggio ; what he was doing was attempting to revive a popular tradition not yet extinct but on the wane for a century or more. He was harking back to St John of the Cross and the *Spiritual Exercises* of St Ignatius Loyola. But sainthood alarms the ordinary man and an art made for saints was bound to cause scandal and offense.

Indeed, the man himself was a target for scandal ; he was constantly quarrelling with his friends on the most trivial grounds,

CARAVAGGIO (1573-1610). THE MARTYRDOM OF ST MATTHEW. CA. 1595. DETAIL. CHURCH OF SAN LUIGI DEI FRANCESI, ROME.

Horror-stricken, the little boy is trying to escape from the sight of the martyred victim, but is too terrified to utter the cry that rises to his lips. Its volumes clearly outlined by the surrounding mass of shadow, the face is reduced (by a procedure subsequently followed by Cézanne) to an oval containing three other ovals, the eyes and mouth : pools of shadow whose mystery is stressed by the two horizontal bars of the eyebrows and the perpendicular of the nose.

This picture was made at the same time as the *Crucifixion of St Paul* for the Cerasi Chapel of S. Maria del Popolo. If Baglione is to be trusted, this is a second version of the same theme which, the first having been 'turned down,' was purchased by Cardinal Sennezio. It belongs to the collection of Princess Vittoria Odescalchi Balbi. The horse, instrument of Providence, fills up all the composition. In the thick, murky atmosphere enveloping the scene, no space is left for the shaft of supernatural light which has struck down the saint. There is not the slightest idealization ; the painter has confined himself to depicting the event as it actually happened, without drawing on his imagination : this in compliance with the new iconographical procedure inaugurated by the Council of Trent. The strongly expressive density we find in this picture is created by lighting which accentuates, here too, the abrupt cessation of all movement. "Caravaggio's realism was, for him, a sort of gospel. It was his conviction that he could impart more veracity to New Testament figures by giving them the faces of his friends than by idealizing them." (André Malraux)

always involved in lawsuits, as ready with his dagger as with the brush. He only avoided prison by making his escape—and this by taking advantage of the hospitality of Prince Colonna and the good offices of Cardinal Gonzaga and the French Ambassador. Caravaggio's reckless temperament was little calculated to make his way an easy one. Indeed, his life was a series of misdeeds and evasions, until at last, after a brief stay at Malta (where he painted Adolf de Wignacourt, Grand Master of the Knights of Malta), he took refuge at Naples, then under Spanish rule. He died at Porto Ercole, in 1610. In his last works—the *Entombment of Santa Lucia*, the *Adoration of the Shepherds* and the *Resurrection of Lazarus*—there are qualities reflecting the storms and stresses of his life, his pent-up grief and bitterness. His output at this time

CARAVAGGIO (1573-1610). THE DEATH OF THE VIRGIN, CA. 1605. DETAIL. LOUVRE, PARIS.

Ordered for the Church of Santa Maria della Scala in Trastevere, this picture was rejected by the Chapter, who found it blasphemous. On Rubens' advice, it was bought by the Duke of Mantua ; in 1627 it found its way into the collection of Charles I of England, then into that of the banker Jabach and, when in 1671 this was sold, into the collection of Louis XIV. This picture caused much scandal, only equaled by the public interest when it was exhibited for a week, at the time when the Duke of Mantua purchased it.

Never before had the Virgin been represented with such realism. The whole composition has a monumental effect, stressed by the violence of the contrasts of light. This is one of the most successful and revealing canvases by Caravaggio that has come down to us.

was prodigious, but hurried, feverish. His composition had become more schematized ; perspective disappeared and a uniform surface served as background, holding the scene together ; the atmosphere thickened and darkened ; the light grew ever duller and its fleeting gleams played only on the few essential figures. But the manner was now broader, bolder, with all retouching gone by the board, and he exaggerated his shadows beyond all natural appearances.

Great painters have no successors ; those who derive from them can do no more than take over their subjects and methods. Caravaggio never had a pupil, but the host of his followers is innumerable. They plundered the heritage he had left, and so shamelessly exploited what they found that Caravaggio's tragic themes became the stock-in-trade of a mere raree-show.

Yet, taking a lead from this dramatic art, one man did find himself. This was Ribera, a Spaniard from Naples, who had vainly sought inspiration from Raphael and Correggio.

Now, under his Spanish hand, Caravaggio's models were turned into wine-swilling dock-workers, the furrows on whose sweaty, grimy faces were the stigmata of their wretched lives. Beneath the rags of his prophets and apostles there lurk, we feel, strange tattoos or scars that they have got in drunken brawls. Ribera is all violence and excess, expressed with rare bravura, whose effect is heightened by the use of an unusually thick, colorful, heavily loaded impasto. The Spaniard adapted himself so well to the taste of his adopted country that such painters as Luca Giordano had to go on turning out his philosophers and old men for many years afterwards to meet the insatiable demand.

Now that his style had 'caught on,' Caravaggio's work was much sought after. Unaware of the secret underlying the painting of this lonely, friendless artist, the buyers relished its pungency and

HENDRICK TER BRUGGHEN (1588-CA. 1629). SHEPHERD PLAYING THE FLUTE (SIGNED AND DATED: H. T. BRUGGHEN FECIT 1621). (27 ½ × 21 ½″) GEMÄLDEGALERIE, CASSEL.

Like Honthorst, Janssens and Bloemaert, his master, Ter Brugghen belonged to the group of the northern followers of Caravaggio; temperamentally, however, he is less akin to Caravaggio than to his disciples, Saraceni and Gentileschi. The known works of Ter Brugghen are dated between 1620 and 1629. Here, the young player's face tells out against a quiet though cheerful, light-hued background. The flute, one would think, has fallen silent, and Ter Brugghen's silence recalls that of La Tour; indeed the influence of the Dutchman on the Lorrainer is obvious, especially in the daylight works. If a shade precious, the treatment here is not particularly skillful, but its poetic quality, the modulations of the local color, the delicacy of the brushwork, the scumbling, and the fine-spun silvery atmosphere justify us in regarding Ter Brugghen as a very great painter.

Designated Apostles or Philosophers, Ribera's figures certainly derive from Caravaggio's aesthetic, but they also reveal the dual influence of Spain and Naples. Colors are warmer, contrasts more violent. The modern literary approach to art—due largely to Hugo's romanticism and Zola's naturalism—incites us to read into Ribera's figures a 'soulfulness' which the Naples dockhands and fishermen, his models, certainly did not possess ; actually this was imposed on the painter by the titles he had to give his pictures, and his customers' taste for the picturesque.

called for ever more heads of St John the Baptist, more ferocious Judiths. And fresh from the lessons of the Carracci, Guido Reni, Domenichino and Guercino, the Bolognese decorators now joined in, like all academic artists whose one concern is not to seem behind the times, and began to 'paint modern,' showering on their perfectly modeled forms the naturalistic lighting of Caravaggio.

But the effect was not always happy, for his conceptions were too new not to deflect the vision of his contemporaries and many of them, whether consciously or not, let themselves be contaminated.

First to be thus affected were the painters of Caravaggio's own generation, even though they had perfected their own technique. Even Rubens—on whose advice the Duke of Mantua bought Caravaggio's *Death of the Virgin*—had to prove to himself that he too could handle contrasts of light and shade with the best of them, as in his *Adoration of the Shepherds*, painted at Rome between 1606 and 1608. But he had sense enough not to keep to a style so little suited to his temperament.

Painters very widely different in background were influenced by the aesthetic of the painter of *The Fortune-Teller* and the *Conversion of St Paul*: Strozzi, from Genoa; Gentileschi, born at Pisa, and inured to Mannerism; Saraceni, a Venetian; and Elsheimer, from Frankfort, all of whom came to Rome at an early date. They all—especially the three last named—worked in a similar vein, so much so that when they treat the same subjects in their smaller pictures, it is difficult to tell them apart. It was Elsheimer who set about introducing Caravaggio's dramatic effects into landscape (an imported form of art).

It was foreign artists who were most susceptible to Caravaggio's influence. Outsiders in Rome, they were less amenable to the local aesthetic tradition. Thus instinctively they turned to the art coming nearest the objective outlook that mediaeval artists had sponsored in their own countries. Thus it was with Finson, Vouet, Valentin, Regnier, Leclerc, Tournier, Baburen, Janssens, Rombouts, Ter Brugghen, Honthorst. Several of them settled for good in Rome and made their careers there. As a result of the esteem these foreigners enjoyed, even Roman artists were infected, and even those who had hitherto stood out against it were forced to adopt Caravaggio's brand of naturalism. His real message gradually lost the force of its meaning, becoming for Manfredi a repertory of themes to plagiarize, and for painters like Preti, Falcone and Galli lo Spadarino, a mere starting-off point for a spate of hollow, melodramatic effects. The religious tone of Caravaggio's art was completely lost; but his style supplied the sauce their 'genre' scenes needed to tickle the palates of a vulgar middle-class public.

Foreign artists in Rome, even those who had come to learn the secrets of Raphael's art, inevitably took home with them a taste for Caravaggio's chiaroscuro. Engraving especially, by its very nature, was the medium that spread 'Caravaggesque' themes all over Europe, and they met with an enthusiastic welcome. One might wonder whether this type of painting, so popular in Lorraine and the North, would have come into existence but for Caravaggio. We cannot doubt, however, that Rembrandt, Vermeer and La Tour would have invented for themselves this 'luminism,' which, in the last analysis, is nowise Italian in spirit. Still it is certain that they found in Caravaggio's art a helpful precedent for their own experiments in light and shadow.

GEORGES DE LA TOUR

Though the traditional stay in Rome became almost obligatory in the second half of the XVIIth century, French painters fell under the spell of Caravaggio only briefly and remembered him just so far as his method of expression corresponded to their own ideas. Such was the case with Simon Vouet, who at an early age went to Venice and then to Rome and, with that capacity for assimilation characteristic of youth, threw himself enthusiastically into the 'dark' manner, like Honthorst, whose methods he seems to have followed. But, as he possessed a wide curiosity and was more concerned with the means of expression suitable to himself than with adopting a manner, he finally returned, like Lanfranc and Guido Reni, to a decorative and narrative style. In 1627, after fourteen years in Rome, he was recalled by Louis XIII and provided tapestry designs and decorations on a large scale for the royal households. Anticipating Lebrun's, his success made him the protagonist of a facile art catering to a policy of prestige. Valentin's attitude was exceptional in the history of French art. Coming to Rome with Vouet, he remained there. Nobody was more like Caravaggio in style or followed him with so much talent. His violent nature was at home in Rome and he is perhaps the only painter of whom it may be said that he lost his French characteristics in Italy. He followed in the footsteps of Manfredi and adopted his themes (fortune-tellers, sharpers, scenes of military life), but for the deep shadows and dark backgrounds of his master, he substituted rich and subtly varied colors, of which the greys and blues demonstrated his preference for the colder tones. At but a slightly lower level than Lebrun's, Valentin's success in France demonstrated the existence of a virile society capable of appreciating full-blooded painting. Louis XIV, that intrepid horseman, keen gambler and hearty eater, had as many as six paintings by Valentin in his room at Versailles. However, the vitality of the French followers of Caravaggio was less suited to Mansart's great gallery than to Gascon manors and the strongholds of the Eastern Marches. After so much anaemic Mannerism, the modern, downright art of Caravaggio's disciples was welcomed in these independent-minded provincial backwaters where Parisian efforts at centralization in politics and art could make no headway. Until 1650, Paris itself was still no more than a big provincial capital and the Academy, recruited from the provincials of the Ile-de-France, had yet, under the sway of Lebrun, to absorb all those groups, which, seen in the false perspective of time, have an air of recalcitrants. There were no provincial schools in the strict sense of the term—except when a strong personality left his mark on the work of his fellow-artists as Tournier did in Toulouse—but rather regional groups. Thus there was the Ile-de-France group, which included Jouvenet, Blanchard, Bourdon, La Hire, Quesnel, Vignon and Michel Corneille. Being exposed to influences as varied as they were mutually contradictory, these painters tended to espouse various aesthetic ideals, those of Bologna, of Venice or even of Caravaggio, as the case might be, and the absence of any common purpose made it all the easier for them to fall under the yoke when Vouet and Lebrun imposed their authority. The Northern group, though also influenced by Italy, preserved the Flemish taste for intimate everyday scenes where man was not merely incidental but the leading subject. This group included Champaigne, Wallerant Vaillant, Bellegambe and the Le Nain brothers. Two distinct groups flourished at the other end of France, namely the Aix group following Finson and including Fauchier, Puget, Brocard and Parrocel, and the Toulouse group including Tournier and Guy François. The latter group was the more independent and homogeneous. Tournier, a pupil of Valentin, settled in Toulouse about 1640. A native of the Franche-Comté, he was trained by a French teacher in Italy and his work is the finest example of the deep originality of the South of France. The predominance of vertical lines and the feeling of stability in his compositions, associated with contrasts of bright reds and deep blacks, have a curiously emotive effect. As a religious painter, Tournier achieved true grandeur and simplicity ; as a painter of battle-scenes, he introduced something new by tackling life-size figures and, in his *Victory of Constantine over Maxentius*, he was not afraid of creating a composition in which there is an astonishing echo of the slow gestures and well-defined masses of the Piero della Francesca fresco at Arezzo, but in a range of colors where purples and greens conflict with the reds. Tournier, Chalette, Durand, François and the Rivalz and de Troy dynasties sufficiently illustrate the independence of a province which did not yet conceive that creative imagination could come from that other 'province' which was Paris, where there was a King with whom the magistrates of Toulouse dealt on equal terms and a quite young Academy which that of the *Jeux floraux* could not yet accept as its superior.

There was yet another group of artists, which, instead of being centered round a particular painter or town, was scattered along the road from the North to Italy, the backbone of the former Lotharingian realm. There, more than anywhere else, Flemish and Southern influences made themselves felt directly and operated in both directions. At Lunéville, there was Georges de La Tour ; at Nancy, Bellange, Lallemand, Callot, Le Clerc, Deruet and Claude ; at Langres, Michelin and the Tassels ; at Dijon, Quentin ; and at Lyons, Le Blanc and Paul Mignard. It was the road of Nicolas Regnier, Ter Brugghen, Rombouts and Van Laer, the road taken by painters from the North and East on their way to Rome, whence they brought back the engravings and procedures of Caravaggio, Saraceni, Gentileschi and Elsheimer.

Georges de La Tour is a disturbing figure to find along this route, because he eludes all definition—so true it is that genius cannot easily be classified, or whittled down to a mere set of influences. A detailed analysis, like M. Pariset's, may elucidate the complex elements of his style, but even when the contribution of Caravaggio through both Saraceni and Jean Le Clerc has been traced and we learn that he may well have made the journey to Italy and worked under Guido Reni in his Caravaggesque period, it brings us no nearer to an understanding of the essential qualities of his art. La Tour was an isolated, little-known figure and, until documents concerning him were discovered, his work was often attributed to Ter Brugghen, Vermeer, Honthorst, Le Nain and even Velazquez, Zurbaran or Rizi ; thus, while his identity was unknown, his merits did not

pass unrecognized. Despite his high esteem today, his fame did not spread beyond the Duchy of Lorraine during his lifetime. A legend given credence by Dom Calmet says that he was painter to the King, who was so enthusiastic about his work that he would have no other paintings in his room. The truth is somewhat simpler. In 1633 Louis XIII was staying at Nancy during the plague epidemic. At that time, it was considered that the best means of escaping a disease was to place oneself under the protection of the saint best equipped to avert it; in this case St Sebastian. La Tour, who specialized in votive paintings of saints, which he duplicated at the request of his buyers, had already painted a St Sebastian for the Duke. He did another for the King, who ordered that all other works of art which might disturb him in his devotions or might offend the Saint himself should be removed from his room. The King's admiration for the painter is merely an assumption, and hardly accords with what we know about the sportsman monarch. The Nancy St Sebastian is the counterpart of Philippe de Champaigne's offering to Notre-Dame de Paris. Both are votive paintings and the title of King's Painter which La Tour subsequently used does not invalidate this opinion. La Tour's fame did not extend beyond his native province, where he was considered as a specialist in sacred art. However astonishing this may appear to us now, it should be remembered that the Douanier Rousseau and Séraphine might have met with a similar fate, if an extraordinary chain of circumstances had not brought them to light. The peculiar greatness of La Tour, which put him beyond any particular school or doctrine, lay in his expression of his unsophisticated soul and the mystic quality of his inspiration. The influences at work are so difficult to verify that he must be approached with infinite care. Chronology is of no avail, but a study of the background helps us to a surer understanding of his art. One observation

GEORGES DE LA TOUR (1593-1652). THE NEWBORN BABE. (30 × 35¾″) RENNES MUSEUM.

First attributed to G. Schalken and then to the Le Nains (1859). The schematic layout is significant spiritually as well as geometrically. Balancing the massive pyramid whose front is an isosceles triangle, its base being the child's body, is the form of the maidservant ; beyond the linking shadow of her hand, she repeats side-face, as if in a play of mirrors, the mother's face.

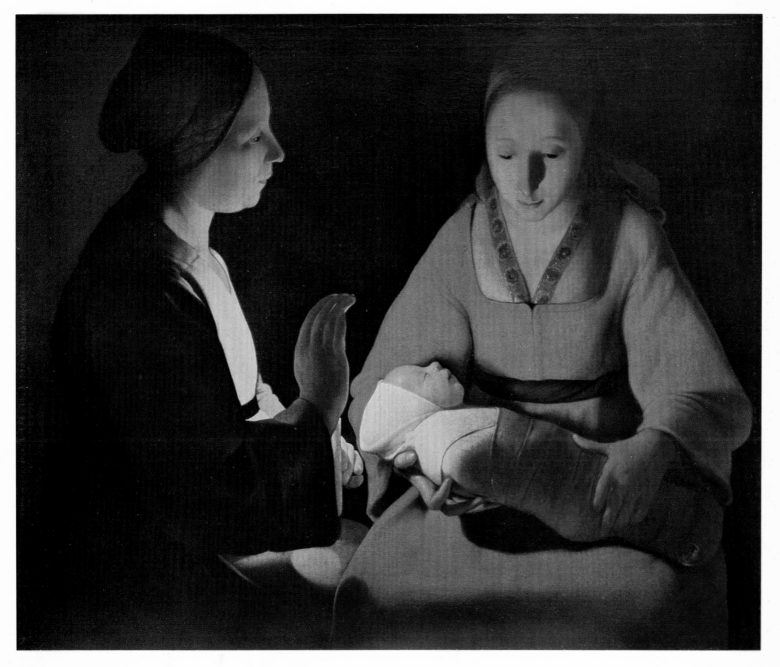

GEORGES DE LA TOUR (1593-1652). MAGDALEN WITH THE LAMP. BETWEEN 1625 and 1633. (50 ¼ × 37″) LOUVRE, PARIS.

The theme of the Magdalen in meditation is a synthesis of two equally popular and widespread themes, namely Melancholy and Vanity. Very many influences are here: the Caravaggesque Italy of Saraceni, Artemesia Gentileschi, Preti and Finson, the Spain of Ribera, the Germany of Dürer and the Flanders of Ter Brugghen and Bloemaert. But purely La Tour's is the mystic feeling of this poignant dialogue between the penitent and God, in the contemplation of Death. Here we have the completely unforced mysticism conjured up by Sponde's famous lines:

Mes yeux ne lancez plus votre pointe éblouie
Sur les brillants rayons de la flammeuse vie.
Sillez-vous, couvrez-vous de ténèbres, mes yeux.

"My eyes, no longer turn your dazzled look
"On the bright radiance of flaming life,
"Be covered up with shadows, O my eyes!"

"The vermilion of the short skirt, the tunic in creamy white with touches of reddish-brown revealing the bruised shoulders, the light flowing over the hand which follows the shape of the skull placed on the knees, the amazing still life formed by the two books, the scourge, the plain wooden cross and the brown oil on the translucent water of the lamp, the tint of the skin under the light, the faint golden glints on the black hair so like a nun's veil: how rich in intimations all these are! The half-hidden face of the Magdalen, gazing beyond the flame towards another world, her head propped on her hand as though bowed by an unbearable weight, the renunciation shown in the attitude of the body, all demonstrate La Tour's deep knowledge of the life of the penitent and mystic, the sacrifices it involves and the 'Dark Night' described by St John of the Cross, in which the soul stripped bare of all, even of its faith, communes with God." (Th. Bertin-Mourot.)

must be made at the outset. All his religious paintings are nocturnes and it is here that he would seem at first sight to be influenced by Caravaggio—which, however, is not the case. His daylight scenes are genre paintings which at first remind us of Flemish painters such as Ter Brugghen and Honthorst, and yet it is in them that he comes nearest to Caravaggio. Whereas the master who gave us *The Vocation of St Matthew* saw religious subjects from a dramatic standpoint, staging his scene at the crucial moment and arranging his lights and shadows to stress the most dramatic incident, La Tour treated his religious themes as timeless happenings, part of an endless cycle, bathed in the silence of prayer. Caravaggio's lighting was a convenient stage-effect, but it was not so with La Tour. Though a candle appears in every case, it is not just as an accessory, but as the subject and almost the purpose of the picture, symbolizing, like the sanctuary lamp, the Divine Presence. The shadowy setting in which Caravaggio placed his saints and martyrs was arbitrary, but with La Tour such settings were an expression of the inmost soul, of that form of devotion which can manifest itself to the full only in the gloom of a dimly-lighted chapel. Caravaggio's world is a closed one from which it is impossible to escape; La Tour's is even more confined, but the flame that burns in it opens up celestial vistas. Between Caravaggio and La Tour lies all the difference between sacred drama and mystic emotion. Such mysticism in an expression rather than a derivative of that simple faith with which the Franciscans of Lorraine and St François Fourrier approached God directly, trustfully, almost familiarly, in their devotions. How far removed is this from the clumsy, almost embarrassing piety of such a painter as Le Sueur!

The effect of La Tour's message is doubtless due to the remarkable extent to which his style is adapted to his thought, which is abstract, yet confident; ingenuously simple, yet profound and wholly mediaeval. Though the composition is perfect, the drawing is often lax and commonplace, but the defects of this inspired primitive are rendered unimportant by his emotional power.

The success of Georges de La Tour would be less easy to understand if our perception had not been purified by Cubism, for

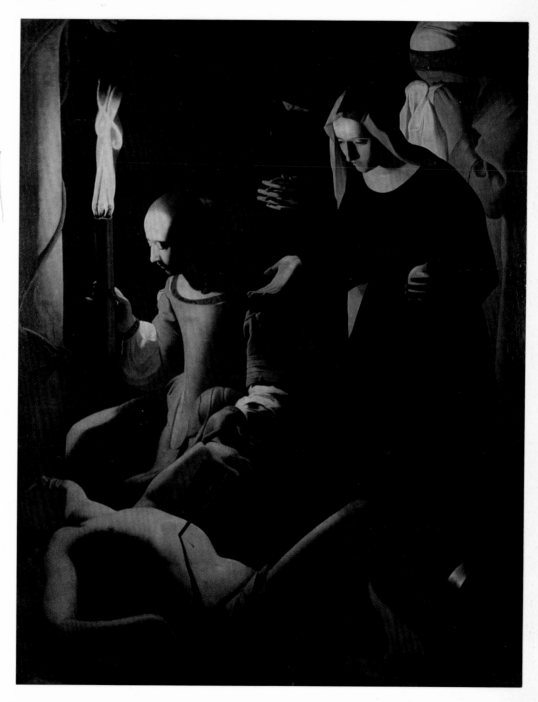

GEORGES DE LA TOUR (1593-1652). ST SEBASTIAN MOURNED BY ST IRENE, 1640-1650. (63 × 50¾") KAISER FRIEDRICH MUSEUM, BERLIN.

G. de La Tour may be said to have specialized in paintings of St Sebastian and it is probable that further versions, in addition to those at Honfleur and Evreux, are yet to be discovered of the Rouen picture and also of that at Berlin.

This group of women saints is treated in the manner of the primitives, and La Tour owes much less to Caravaggio than to the French genius as expressed in the Nouans *Pietà*, of Fouquet, from whom he seems to have taken over not only the figures, but the architectural style, the simplicity of volumes and the gravely gentle tone.

The torch is an instrument of overwhelming revelation: "a sort of iris, a vivid orchid, like a piece of exquisitely fashioned glasswork." (L. GILLET.)

the two are intimately connected. Quoting a dictum current in the studios of the Renaissance: "No one can aspire to master-craftsmanship without possessing an expert knowledge of geometry," André Lhote has observed that La Tour's style has qualities which "can only be obtained through a knowledge of geometrical drawing, proportion and the simplification of planes ..." "Construction does not mean the building of dikes to hold in as much earthbound matter as possible. It is rather the setting of subtle snares for the spirit, the erection of a sort of Jacob's ladder to enable the angels within us to escape."

Striking examples of this systematic simplification, where intelligence and sensitivity are subordinated to inspiration, are to be found in our own contemporary art, a case in point being that of La Fresnaye. But, following Cubism and stemming from it, another art, namely that of the poster, has enabled us to understand the necessity of sacrificing form, and the emotive value of color effects. Our age lacks subtlety and obviously has much to learn. La Tour's message is not merely a pictorial one, and its truth is all the more impressive and salutary, if we can also perceive the mystery implicit in it.

2
COLOR, TEXTURE, EMOTION

VELAZQUEZ - LOUIS LE NAIN

IN HOLDING *up a mirror to reality, the program he had set himself, Caravaggio placed his figures in an artificial lighting intended to bring out traits of character—a method which risked developing into a mere artistic 'trick.' But the painters soon rebelled against the presence of any intermediary between them and the real world. There was a vastly greater field of visual experience in direct observation of nature, of human faces as they appear in the ever-changing light of every day. In his early phase, Velazquez still fell back on allegory to justify the inclusion in his pictures of scenes of domestic life, the gestures of the peasant or the workman. But his art evolved so rapidly that, by the time he had become a court painter, he painted kings and princes like ordinary men and treated landscape without embellishments. It was left to a humble French provincial, Louis Le Nain, to give the world a rendering, never to be surpassed, of rustic life in all its simple dignity. As was to happen again when Impressionism came to the fore, the technique of these artists, as they progressively shook off convention, grew purer and more luminous; discarding needless shadows, the drab, compounded colors of the art school, they lit on delicate nuances, pinks, pale blues and greys, the natural colors of vibrant air.*

SONORITY OF VELAZQUEZ

The impetus given to Spain under Charles V lasted on into the reign of Philip II, but by then had almost spent its force. The façade was splendid, but delusive. Spanish literature had entered on its great period with Cervantes, Gongora and Lope de Vega, and there were painters of no less importance : El Greco, Ribera, Velazquez, Zurbaran and Murillo. The cracks in the crumbling structure were hidden from contemporaries by its brilliant surface ; but a nation cannot be carried along by the same impulse for ever. The century, dazzled by the glories of Spanish art, failed to sense the approaching dissolution of the old Hapsburg Empire.

In 1599, the year when Cervantes wrote *Don Quixote*, Van Dyck, Painter in Ordinary to be to Charles I of England, was born in Antwerp, and Diego Rodriguez da Silva y Velazquez, Court Painter to be to Philip IV of Spain, was born in Seville. Spanish art had shown very little originality throughout the greater part of the XVIth century, if we except Berruguete's polychromatic sculptures. Sanchez Coello, the most notable of the painters, was primarily a draftsman and, like the Clouets in France, he succeeded in penetrating the characters of his models simply by a detailed, sensitive portrayal of their features. With Coello and his successor Pantoja de la Cruz, a tradition of the psychological portrait and the court portrait was established, paving the way for Velazquez, even if the means employed were still limited and austere.

It remained for El Greco to appear on the scene bringing the best of the technique of the Venetian painters, their skillful handling of color freed from all formalism, their daring directness and sense of values. The amazing thing was that this foreigner, who absorbed the spirit of his adopted country sufficiently to be indistinguishable from its own sons, should have dropped all decorative or external considerations at his first contact with it. While he was quick to rebuff Philip II, when the latter summoned him to the Escorial, he succeeded in keeping up friendly relations with the intellectual, noble and religious *élite* of the imperial city of Toledo. This is borne out by the celebrated interview reported by Pacheco and published in Seville, in 1647. And Pacheco was the master and subsequently the father-in-law of Velazquez.

Thus it was the latter began by familiarizing himself with the Venetian painters, whose major works he was later to find in the royal collections, which were especially rich in Titians acquired by Charles V, who had dreamed in vain of establishing the painter, in whom he had found such an outstanding chronicler, in Spain. "The good and the beautiful," wrote Velazquez, "are to be found in Venice, and Titian is their standard-bearer."

Few painters have made an easier start in life than Velazquez ; his vocation was manifested in his early youth, when he was studying classics, in his urge to draw and his particular fondness for scientific observation and the austere discipline of mathematics. His artistic tendencies were encouraged by his family and, at the age of thirteen, he was apprenticed to the best painter in Seville, Herrera el Viejo, who was renowned for his bold and brutal style. But this teacher, an unamiable, irascible man, soon got on the nerves of his young pupil, who left him for Pacheco, who encouraged the taste of Velazquez and his fellow-pupils, Zurbaran and Alonso Cano, for faithful representation. Pacheco is not remembered as a painter, but, like Gustave Moreau, as a teacher who recognized the abilities of his pupils and helped them on their way. He was a liberal-minded master, who professed "to hold to nature in everything." Velazquez thus began by applying himself to a meticulous analysis of the objects forming his 'bodegons,' still lifes with simple volumes, the texture and density of which he reproduced, while being careful not to make so much a photographic copy as a sublimation of his visual experience. He was obsessed by the ideal of relief and by Pacheco's advice: "The picture should stand forth from the frame," though he was less interested in 'the picture' than in interpreting form. To those who were surprised at his disdain for the Mannerists, Velazquez retorted that "he would rather be first in the rustic, than second in the delicate manner." And indeed his earliest works showed perfect mastery of execution, but his portraits, always of the same models, the valet and the old servant, were rather exercises in the play of lights and shadows than studies of expression. When expression existed, it was only incidental. Though the water-carrier in his fawn leather waistcoat is apparently of no more importance than the jug or glass of water he holds, he too exists in his own right, if in an elementary way. Thus the painter, by his devotion to accuracy and his practice of analysis, had already gained exceptional means of expression, before starting to bring the same curiosity to bear on the man's inner self as he brought to bear on his appearance. Yet can those first attempts be related to the work of Caravaggio and his school without stretching a point ? We have no reason to believe that Caravaggio was known in Seville before 1617, and the influence of Ribera cannot be alleged, as he did not settle in Naples until 1620 and, according to Justi, none of his works reached Spain before 1631. It was in their rejection of the fashionable Mannerist outlook that the two painters were akin to one another ; but they were quite different in their interests and techniques. In his 'luminist' compositions, Caravaggio always arranged the sacred scene with obvious apologetic intentions, which are scarcely felt in the Velazquez painting of Jesus in the home of Martha and Mary. This interior in the manner of Peter Aertsen, set strangely enough in a kitchen, gives the impression rather of a painting hanging on the wall than of a real scene observed through a window ; obviously the luminous atmosphere bathing objects still eluded the painter. Still we must remember he was only eighteen and had, anyhow, achieved his juvenile ambition "to be the first in the rustic manner."

Such exceptional beginnings pointed to a successful future, but not necessarily an official career, and the subsequent events may seem astonishing in the case of a young painter who set such narrow limits on his talent. Was it chance or deliberate ambition that in 1623 took Velazquez to Madrid, where he was welcomed by his father-in-law's friend, Don Juan Fonseca, who introduced him to the Court with a recommendation to Duke Olivarez ? Velazquez was twenty-three years of age when he became Court Painter and started his career as an exemplary official, who, over a period of thirty-seven

For Velazquez, still lifes and faces alike were simply pretexts for depicting the varied play of light. The still life has a rigorous symmetry, resembling the more allusive symmetry of Zurbaran's 'bodegons.' We see the artist's plan in the way he has set off the pairs of eggs and the fishes, with their play of curves and ovals, against the rigid structure of the imbricated rectangles of the picture illustrating the gospel story.

years, was to paint, in his top-floor studio at the Alcazar, over eighty-three portraits of members of the royal family, over sixty of courtiers, some twenty large religious and mythological subjects, portraits of jesters and dwarfs, landscapes and hunting-scenes, in addition to carrying out his duties at the court. He served in turn as Gentleman Usher, Officer of the Wardrobe, Groom of the Bedchamber, Chamberlain and Assistant Supervisor of Royal Architecture, Inspector of Buildings, and finally, in 1652, Grand Marshal of the Palace. This uniformly successful official career was an astonishing one for a painter of talent and might suggest a genius for backstairs intrigue more than one for color and drawing. There is a sort of latent incompatibility between the words 'career,' 'painting' and 'official.' The example of Lebrun, who had a similar career in the same century, goes to show that one cannot serve two masters and that the painter cannot please both himself and his patron. Velazquez' work is either an exception to this rule or else disproves it.

Through the force of circumstances rather than a natural bent, Velazquez thus became a portraitist and a court portraitist at that. Actually, however, the painter, still

under the influence of his early studies, regarded his royal subjects in the same manner as Cézanne regarded his apples. He was little interested in the psychology of his model and was moreover too prudent at the outset of his career to risk trying to reveal the inmost feelings of Philip IV. He was content with faithfulness to appearance, yet this very accuracy served to convey, unknown to himself and without deliberate intent, the heredity of his royal model, whose face reveals tenderness, a will constantly held in check by scruples and, most of all, an acute sense of his own ineffectiveness.

All day long, whenever he had leisure from his other duties, Velazquez painted. Without imagination, but with scrupulous accuracy, he painted the royal children, courtiers, dwarfs and jesters. There was nothing in him of the repressed feelings of a Ruy Blas who took revenge on the society surrounding him by cruelly emphasizing its blemishes. That 'vain romanticism' which has been attributed to him was absolutely foreign to his

VELAZQUEZ (1599-1660).
THE WATER-CARRIER, CA. 1620.
(41½ × 32¼") COLLECTION OF THE
DUKE OF WELLINGTON, LONDON.

The rendering of volume interested Velazquez; this scene, too, is a pretext for a combination of ovoid forms. Note the turning movement of the pitchers, cups and faces. Its realism notwithstanding, this scene is treated from a purely painterly, not a psychological angle; figures are painted with the same feeling for surface texture as the objects, the tanned skin has the same physical density as the thick earthenware of the pitchers.

(NOT NATURALIST)

talent. His so-called realism was devoid of any ulterior motive. It is surely wrong to call a painter a realist when he is satisfied simply with the truth expressed by things, and to assume that this objectivity is only a veil concealing some deep-seated rancor. Velazquez, judging by his painting, had not the soul of a lackey, and the tenderness of his portraits of the Infantas expressed something more than the feelings of a courtier. While the portrait of Olivarez shows a swashbuckler rather than a brilliant officer (was this flattery or satire ?), Velazquez painted him without the least irony, if only because he could not paint otherwise. Like Manet, who was to admire him so much, Velazquez was an eye and nothing but an eye.

His career might have followed an unruffled course and would already have been

TITIAN (1477-1576). THE PRESENTATION IN THE TEMPLE, 1534-1538. DETAIL. ACADEMY, VENICE.

Asked about Italian painting by Salvator Rosa, Velazquez said : "The good and the beautiful are to be found in Venice, and Titian is their standard-bearer." He discerned in Venetian painting what he was seeking for and soon to achieve : a sort of scientific dissection of the subject, and an analysis of the visible world in terms of color.

1718

44

(NOT NATURALIST)

talent. His so-called realism was devoid of any ulterior motive. It is surely wrong to call a painter a realist when he is satisfied simply with the truth expressed by things, and to assume that this objectivity is only a veil concealing some deep-seated rancor. Velazquez, judging by his painting, had not the soul of a lackey, and the tenderness of his portraits of the Infantas expressed something more than the feelings of a courtier. While the portrait of Olivarez shows a swashbuckler rather than a brilliant officer (was this flattery or satire?), Velazquez painted him without the least irony, if only because he could not paint otherwise. Like Manet, who was to admire him so much, Velazquez was an eye and nothing but an eye.

His career might have followed an unruffled course and would already have been

TITIAN (1477-1576). THE PRESENTATION IN THE TEMPLE, 1534-1538. DETAIL. ACADEMY, VENICE.

Asked about Italian painting by Salvator Rosa, Velazquez said: "The good and the beautiful are to be found in Venice, and Titian is their standard-bearer." He discerned in Venetian painting what he was seeking for and soon to achieve: a sort of scientific dissection of the subject, and an analysis of the visible world in terms of color.

under the influence of his early studies, regarded his royal subjects in the same manner as Cézanne regarded his apples. He was little interested in the psychology of his model and was moreover too prudent at the outset of his career to risk trying to reveal the inmost feelings of Philip IV. He was content with faithfulness to appearance, yet this

very accuracy served to convey, unknown to himself and without deliberate intent, the heredity of his royal model, whose face reveals tenderness, a will constantly held in check by scruples and, most of all, an acute sense of his own ineffectiveness.

All day long, whenever he had leisure from his other duties, Velazquez painted. Without imagination, but with scrupulous accuracy, he painted the royal children, courtiers, dwarfs and jesters. There was nothing in him of the repressed feelings of a Ruy Blas who took revenge on the society surrounding him by cruelly emphasizing its blemishes. That 'vain romanticism' which has been attributed to him was absolutely foreign to his

VELAZQUEZ (1599-1660).
THE WATER-CARRIER, CA. 1620.
(41½ × 32¼″) COLLECTION OF THE
DUKE OF WELLINGTON, LONDON.

The rendering of volume interested Velazquez; this scene, too, is a pretext for a combination of ovoid forms. Note the turning movement of the pitchers, cups and faces. Its realism notwithstanding, this scene is treated from a purely painterly, not a psychological angle; figures are painted with the same feeling for surface texture as the objects, the tanned skin has the same physical density as the thick earthenware of the pitchers.

VELAZQUEZ (1599-1660). THE OMELETTE, CA. 1618. DETAIL. COOK COLLECTION, LOANED TO THE FITZWILLIAM
MUSEUM, CAMBRIDGE, ENGLAND.

enough to ensure his fame, had not the coming of Rubens started him on a new path. Rubens, who was on an official mission, stayed at the Escorial from August 1628 to April 1629 and shared Velazquez' studio. He was then fifty and at the height of his genius. He appreciated his junior and taught him the science of composition and of rendering space, expression and movement. His influence had an immediate effect, but, strictly speaking, lasted for only one picture. That famous work, *The Topers*, dates from this period and shows an attentive pupil, somewhat like Jordaens, though with greater balance, and, by an odd reversion, echoing the generalized types of Hals. Rubens encouraged Velazquez and urged the King to let his painter make the indispensable journey to Italy. The route he took during the years 1629 and 1630 is well-known, but Rome and Venice captivated him most. He rediscovered Titian and Tintoretto, made studies of the *Crucifixion* and copied *The Communion of the Apostles*. His contact with Tintoretto may have been responsible for the new atmosphere of his paintings : a greater diffusion of light, greyer harmonies, more flexible drawing. He took over Titian's colorful palette, his sensitivity and quickness of touch. But perhaps it is wrong to speak of influences here. It seems rather that

VELAZQUEZ (1599-1660). PORTRAIT OF PHILIP IV, 1636-1638. (78×44″) REPRODUCED BY COURTESY OF THE TRUSTEES, THE NATIONAL GALLERY, LONDON.

One of the most characteristic of Velazquez' great portraits. Here the costume and the materials are treated so freely that they become the most living, most telling, part of the picture ; and the light is rendered with a sort of unconscious *pointillisme*.

VELAZQUEZ (1599-1660). THE
SURRENDER OF BREDA. BEFORE
1635. DETAIL. PRADO, MADRID.

In its treatment, this detail shows
certain tendencies which modern
painting was to turn to good account.
The problem is that of the building
up of form by means of color. Uniform color is replaced by separate,
juxtaposed touches. And the super-
imposed planes suffice, in themselves,
to suggest depth.

a creative instinct, which had long been stifled and needed a change of scene and Italian skies before it could flourish, was set free in Venice, for he had seen works by Titian and Tin-toretto at the Escorial every day and must certainly have been struck by them. *Vulcan's Forge* inaugurated a new manner which was less static, more mindful of effect. His second journey to Italy in 1650, when Philip IV sent him to purchase works for his Academy of Art, further confirmed these tendencies. While he still retained the coldness of the analyst, he freed himself from the complex of objectivity at all costs. He realized that it was possible, without sacri-ficing accurate form, to give that relief, which was his constant preoccupation, a deeper reality through a bolder use of light. The portrait of Pope Innocent X in an extraordinary range of reds saw the application of this new 'luminist' technique. In the Italian landscapes and in those studies of the Villa Medici which he painted for himself, for the mere joy of painting, without reference to the tastes of his clients, he discovered the true value of light and, indeed, in a sense, invented Impressionism. But his humanist background and his habit of working over his subject, returning to it constantly and conscientiously, prevented him from following up a procedure which, in the last analysis, is but a game, we might almost say a 'trick.' He employed this rapid placing of lights and colors only in his backgrounds and details, and for the garments of his models, thus giving his portraits as it were a vibrant

VELAZQUEZ (1599-1660). PORTRAIT OF PHILIP IV, 1636-1638. DETAIL. REPRODUCED BY COURTESY OF THE TRUSTEES, THE NATIONAL GALLERY, LONDON.

Color has no secrets for Velazquez. Sometimes he creates delicate nuances and the softly blended tones have an almost musical effect. Or he subordinates the color of details to building up the *ensemble* in terms of light. He often worked out-of-doors, as we see from these portraits obviously painted in the open air. Manet, too, was to acquire in the open air that understanding of light which the Impressionists turned to good account.

VELAZQUEZ (1599-1660). THE WEAVERS, CA. 1657. DETAIL. PRADO, MADRID.

When he deals with 'popular' subjects Velazquez uses a quite different style. The almost geometrical lay-out of this picture enables him to emphasize the masses of color on which the light is playing. These blocks of color make a direct attack on our senses and give the scene intense reality. The forms have the forthrightness of a Courbet portrait, while in the distribution of the light we have a foretaste of Renoir.

accompaniment of warmth and music. At the pinnacle of his career, he realized that his objectivity was only an illusion, all the more regrettable in that his attention to form and volume had hindered him from seeing that true form which is the very essence, the soul, of things. His last big compositions, *Las Meninas* and *The Weavers*, were no longer the literal reproduction of a *milieu* but a personal rendering of myths to which the painter's vision imparts an immanent reality. Technique restricts, but genius transcends it. And in the end Velazquez dared to re-create the world within him. "The soul of the artist contains objective reality ; and this proves the supremacy of spirit over matter." As Charles de Tolnay has said, the soul of Velazquez in *Las*

Meninas contains reality and its visible projection in a semi-impressionist technique. He seems to anticipate that notion of the picture as a 'state of mind', for this canvas is the reflection of an inner spiritual vision ; no mere imitation of the obvious reality. Here perhaps we have an indication of the drama underlying the triumphant progress of Velazquez' career. His position as a court official seemed to invite submission to the tastes and whims of his royal master and like Lebrun he might have devoted his genius to extolling the pomp and power of the monarchy. But, true Spaniard that he was, Velazquez stood fiercely by his freedom of judgment and his artistic conscience. Moreover his innate liking for rustic scenes discouraged him from any social or aesthetic compromise with his environment. In the whole history of painting there has been no other master to whom that somewhat overworked description of painting as a 'language' created by the artist so well applies. His palette has all the charm, all the suavity of a completely euphonious voice ; perfectly clear, never in the least affected, it is a natural gift and, as such, intransmissible. Thus he, like Corot and Renoir had would-be followers, but none could carry on the torch ; this, indeed, has been the fate of many another great and solitary artist. Renoir showed his awareness of this when he said : "What I like so much in Velazquez is that aristocratic touch one finds in all he does, down to the least detail, in a mere ribbon ... that little pink ribbon of the Infanta Margarita, for example. All the art of painting is incarnate in that ribbon." And his awareness of this probably explains the mystery of Velazquez' 'spiritual realism.'

Las Meninas (1656) and *The Weavers* (1657) were Velazquez' last contribution to the world's art. He died in 1660. His is a place apart, unique, in the history of painting. His distant heirs, Manet, Degas and Monticelli, were to invoke his example and borrow his methods, but to respect his lonely eminence. For to all those who looked to him for inspiration and silent counsel, he seemed to be indeed the first lord of painters—the artist's eye and the craftsman's hand were his in their supreme degree. His art stood beyond the glass of fashion, taste and chance. No school could claim him, no 'genre' restrict his serene genius. The time came when all schools drew on the abundant, many-sided heritage he left them, and the lessons of his mastery were at once their admiration and despair.

We may say that, of all XVIIth-century painters, Velazquez was the one whose impact on the art to come was the most difficult to foresee. When he died in 1660, twenty years after Rubens, nine years before Rembrandt, the legacy of his incomparable art fell to no one ; he had neither disciple nor successor. It was at this time that the primacy of Italian painting had at last worked to its close, while in France artists were in power whose aim it was to make the picture 'show something' : hence the popularity of the portrait and the 'genre' scene. Velazquez had been, to an even greater degree than Veronese and Titian, a pure painter, unconstrained by the demands of the subject. And this it was, two hundred years later, that Manet learned from him, the lesson he in turn passed on to all modern art : that the picture, in itself, contains its own reality, that it is not for painting to figure forth the world around us, but to transform that world into painting. The artist was no longer to hold the world for a valid reality—or even an apparent reality—to which artistic expression should be subordinated. No longer responsible for a rendering of the forms of reality as we usually conceive them, but setting out now to create an order solely in the interests of the picture, painting metamorphosed standard conceptions of sensation and bent emotion to her own exacting ends. From this time on—at least for a painter of Velazquez' peerless gifts—restrictions of this kind ceased to exist ; the forms of the visible world no longer restrained his creative will. A new way lay open when painting came thus to have no more tangible a subject than do musical compositions. A picture became the projection in space of an inward reality of the painter's own, not perforce reflecting the meaning of, or even representing, what the eye might see. Here we could dwell at length on the example offered by *Las Meninas* : is it a portrait of the artist, a court portrait, a 'genre' scene ? Definitions of this kind fall away. All that remains is a moment of time suspended between the past and the future, pregnant with abstract intimations that flicker from face to face across the picture. Each face is an essential object, an essential sign into which we may attempt to read the only meaning of the picture. In the last analysis, neither the subject in itself, nor the attitudes of the figures, nor the underlying aims of the artist have any importance : their world, its time, space and circumstance refined away, has become a picture.

LOUIS LE NAIN

As against Velazquez, the Le Nain brothers cut the figure of *petits maîtres*. How could those humble French countryfolk they loved to paint fail to seem even more insignificant when contrasted with the great figures of the court of Philip IV ? Yet, despite its pomp and luxury and its serene confidence in the power of birth and money, was not the grandeur that was Spain founded on an illusion ? The monarchy at Madrid was riding for a fall ; his Most Christian Majesty had counted on the Church to see him through, but Providence had sided with the Protestant Republic of the Low Countries. And the art of Spain was declining on Gongorism and the effeminate graces of Murillo. Meanwhile France kept her doors open to foreign influences and was growing conscious of the great part she was to play in European culture. The high-handed procedure of the Hapsburgs in driving out the Jews and Moors had broken up the industrial and commercial bourgeoisie, whereas the liberalism of Laffemas and Richelieu favored the rise to power of the middle class. Thus Spain was being brought to ruin by her blind nationalism and authoritarian ideology, while France, thanks to her wider outlook and freedom of mind, was enjoying great prosperity. For many generations the paintings of the Le Nains figured in French history books as illustrations of the new social groups— peasants, rustics and obscure country gentlefolk—amongst whom the Bourbons recruited their civil service, thus pointing the way to modern France. And obviously an artist whose works served only to grace the pages of history books could hardly be taken seriously. Indeed it seemed that, once the School of Fontainebleau had gained favor, French art had become emasculated and that the national tradition had died with Fouquet, leaving the field free for Italy. Yet, although rulers had changed and with them the official art, the native genius of the country was unaffected.

France had come of age in the XVIIth century and the figures depicted by the Le Nains reflect this new responsibility. While clearly conscious of their new-found stature, they are dubious as to what posterity may think of them ; but they have a sense of duty. They are moral beings who do not shirk their problems. Convinced of the greatness of their mission, they make no attempt to avoid it. Lebrun and Vouet might paint history, but they already *are* history.

The disturbances in France at the end of the XVIth century scarcely favored the arts, and painting found a refuge in the immediate circle of the King at Paris and Fontainebleau, or among the bankers at Lyons. Artists without commissions—the churches were destroyed or desecrated and the castles burnt—had fled to Italy and settled there. They had lost contact with the stricken and unhappy reality that was France and found an empty inspiration in mythology and the fantastic. Montaigne waxed indignant. "We should make art natural as thoroughly as they (the painters) make nature artificial." And later Malherbe struck the same note. "The porters of the Port au Foin have everything to teach us about language." And why not about art, too ? The Le Nains, solid provincials from Laon, were not given to doctrine or theory,

LOUIS LE NAIN (1593-1648). THE FORGE (FRAGMENT). LOUVRE, PARIS.

"The scene is set in front of the forge, whose blaze lights up the background of the picture and is reflected on the faces grouped around it. All these simple folk with their naïve, expressive faces have only one fault and it can easily be condoned : they are all turned towards the spectator." (SAINTE-BEUVE)

This picture 'features' much the same characters as the family meals and similar groups, but the reflected light adds to the poetic quality of this scene from life Its date is unknown, but it is probably earlier than the *Forge* at Rheims, in which Mathieu Le Nain aspired to the mythological, with a Venus in the Italian manner and timid attempts at heroic nudity. It has been ingeniously suggested that Mathieu visited Rome in 1630, when Velazquez was painting the *Vulcan's Forge* there. An attractive hypothesis, but is it really called for ?

LOUIS LE NAIN (1593-1648). PEASANT FAMILY IN AN INTERIOR, CA. 1643. (44 ½ × 62 ½″) LOUVRE, PARIS.

The farmer's family is grouped around the table in the order of precedence still observed by the French peasantry of today. Only the father is really sitting at the table, for he is the lord and master, the head of the family tired after a long day's work and to him deference is due. The women are snatching a bite between their errands to and from the fireplace, dresser and cellar. The glass of wine in the mother's hand has probably just been filled and she is going to set it before her husband with the jug of fresh water, but for a moment she has ceased bustling round the table. The eldest daughter, seated sideways, keeps her father company, while the children stay around waiting to eat with the women. The little boy is playing a flute to while away the time. The painter's visit seems to have caught them by surprise and all movement is arrested ; the father has put down his knife, the mother pauses before rising, the flute is silent. They look at the newcomer in the same way as a laborer stops reaping and a farmer's wife stops churning, when something catches their eye.

Yet, despite the wonderful lifelikeness of the scene, quite likely the actual painting was done in the artist's studio, each character posing separately.

It would be rash to attribute the Le Nains to the lineage of Caravaggio. No doubt they came to know of him through other painters who had been to Rome, but the technical achievements of the great Italian would have struck them as less important than the moral significance they sought to give their work.

but they rebelled instinctively against the showy trivialities of Jean Cousin and Toussaint Dubreuil, just as that other provincial, Caravaggio, had rebelled against Vanni, Zuccaro and Baroccio. They tried not so much to renew painting as to protest against academic superficiality : the game had become too easy, the moves too obvious.

54

Their world was a simple one and the Flemish folk artists had shown them that models taken from everyday life were more convenient to paint and that genre scenes found a readier market than altarpieces. Moreover reality is always a rich hunting-ground for the unimaginative.

Yet if they lacked imagination, the Le Nains were poets. Though they were painters of reality, they were not realists in our sense of the word. For them, reality consisted in whatever could be grasped quickly and effortlessly. With a gravity tinged with melancholy, they depicted the age-old dream of the countryman : that there should be peace to ripen the wheat, fill the barns and provide bread and wine, that wars should cease and love be chaste. To be intelligible and thus communicable, the dream had to be clothed in an outward and visible form. "Reality is in the soul and in certain rare and simple souls this reality is called poetry." With the Le Nains, as

with La Tour, their spiritual aspirations ranged further than problems of technique, but they always tried to treat their subject matter in a painterly manner, for, like poetry, their painting is a language—a language whose secret we have lost, but which contemporaries understood. These meals of peasants are simply transpositions on to a homelier plane of the Last Supper or that at Emmaus, so thoroughly religious is their atmosphere. These tables are altars where bread is broken and wine is drunk, while the guests are conscious of performing a sacred rite, humble witnesses to the mystery of life. But, in addition to this spiritual message, so characteristic of the XVIIth century, with its strong religious bias, the

LOUIS LE NAIN (1593-1648). PEASANT FAMILY IN AN INTERIOR, CA. 1643. DETAIL. LOUVRE, PARIS.

From the face of the old woman with the glass of wine emanates the tranquil strength, the serenity, that only simple, sincere faith can inspire. This face constitutes a link between the Avignon *Pietà* with its donor, a countryman and a believer, and Cézanne's peasants.

A century later we find the same quality of color, the same richly human *matière* and inner warmth in Chardin's still lifes, especially in his *Pipes et vases à boire*, where the objects have the same homely familiarity as the peasant woman's face. Chardin brings to the still life the same deep sympathy as that between Le Nain and his sitter.

LOUIS LE NAIN (1593-1648). THE CART. (22×28 ¼″) (SIGNED AND DATED ON A TREE-TRUNK AT BOTTOM, LEFT: LE NAIN FECIT 1641) LOUVRE, PARIS.

A peasant woman sitting in the foreground, partly against the light, suckles her baby. Four children, perched on the cart 'hold the pose.' Farther away, two little girls seem to be chatting with the little swineherd. All three groups are held in a fragile equilibrium. At a sign, the whole skillful composition would collapse and the children scatter, running and laughing.

It is interesting to note that in each of Le Nain's compositions there is a leading figure, through whom the picture seems to be looking at us, and on whom the lay-out centers. Here the whole life of the scene is concentrated in the peasant-woman with the child in her arms, in the foreground; all the rest is *décor*, all the others are 'extras.' In any other painter's hands this plethora of subjects and objects of all kinds would have led the way to Baroque. But Le Nain holds faithfully to his principle of simplicity, forthrightness, and knows the secret of achieving these even in a crowded canvas.

paintings of the Le Nains embody certain abiding features of the French character. The austerity and asceticism which we find in the *Peasant Family in an Interior* may take us by surprise, yet it is none the less in keeping with the love of life displayed by these poor farm laborers at table. The child playing the flute is typically French in his sweetness and joy, and recurs in the paintings of Chardin and Millet. The mother's whole attitude suggests harshness, touched with grief. This apparent harshness is due to a certain gravity of treatment, an asceticism of form which we also find in the master of the Avignon Pietà, in Cézanne and Gauguin.

In the last analysis, what we call realism in the Le Nains is their search for essentials, their cult of truth, their desire for simplicity and their passion for purity and, generally speaking, these are national characteristics of French painting and the French spirit.

For a long time, no distinction was drawn between the members of the family; indeed the art of each of the Le Nain brothers, Antoine, Louis and Mathieu, is complementary to that of the two others. While modern criticism may attempt to give each his due, art history has lumped them together indiscriminately. For once then let us defer to the critics, for it was they who rescued the Le Nain brothers from oblivion. In 1862, their fellow-countryman Champfleury first drew attention to them, but it was Sir Robert C. Witt who organized the first large-scale exhibition of their work, which took place at the Burlington Fine Arts Club in 1910, and made an attempt at classification. In 1922-1923, Paul Jamot reviewed the problem, but the solutions he advanced, impressive though they were, failed to convince M. Davis and G. Isarlo completely. Finally Josephine M. Lansing has suggested the existence of a fourth Le Nain. The issue is still confused; but perhaps the descriptive catalogue of the work of each of the brothers, which G. Isarlo has promised us, will throw new light on the subject. Nevertheless, it is possible to discern three different manners in the joint work of the Le Nains. The authorship of some of it is still uncertain, but there is little point in attributing to Antoine, Louis or Mathieu minor works which add nothing to their respective reputations.

Antoine kept very close to the Flemish 'Little Masters'; he retained their old-fashioned, if spirited, execution, and their liking for the picturesque anecdote. He was an optimist who loved the frank, mischievous faces of children, but was also responsive to their moments of charming, almost adult gravity. In this he was akin to Chardin and Manet. He also liked the company of hearty good fellows, pleased with their success in business and apt to prolong the bonhomie of family meals in endless games of cards. However, though he felt most at home in *genre* painting and remained faithful to his Flemish approach to art, Antoine enlarged his scope under the influence of Louis, with whom he collaborated on the famous *Cart*. And his portrait of the Marquis de Trois-villes (1644) proved that he was capable of tackling something bigger.

Of the family trio Louis was the painter *par excellence*. From Aertsen, he learnt the constructive value of light and through him he was attracted towards the Italy of the Bassanos, towards that 'poetry of old age' which he found so moving and which naturally drew him into the orbit of Caravaggio, of whom Gentileschi, during his stay in Paris in 1625, was the best ambassador. But his realism and especially the almost mystical sweep of his inspiration brought him closer to the genius of Spain. The influences he underwent were superficial and served only to confirm him in his own technical methods. His affinities with Velazquez were subtler but struck deeper. Both painters had their roots in an age-old Western tradition, as modified by Christianity. The peasants of Louis Le Nain are not the 'wild beasts' spoken of by La Bruyère, nor are they clodhoppers or yokels, let alone demagogues. They are the aristocrats of the common folk, their strength and pride, 'the salt of the earth.' They have the roughness of bark, the savor of good fruit, the mildness of the ox and the ass. They are ritual figures taking part in the cycle of nature and conscious of their hieratic role. They sit within the arc of a circle and this wonderful stability, together with the simplicity of the composition, so far removed from the 'bambocciata'—the rustic, naturalistic *genre* piece introduced into Rome about 1626 by Van Laar, nicknamed Il Bamboccio—gives the work an unusual poetic quality, reminiscent of the best of Charles-Louis Philippe, and with something in it of the tender, almost naïve, light of Corot and the pale greys and dull browns of the restrained and sensitive color schemes of Juan Gris and Braque.

Mathieu Le Nain undoubtedly made the journey to Italy. The inspiration he gained from the school of Caravaggio started him on a path which was almost the opposite of that taken by Louis. He was an 'up-to-date' painter specializing in the *genre* scenes made fashionable by Valentin, and also in the court portrait. He changed his brothers' peasants into conventionally pastoral shepherds. The poetry was missing and only the facile, elegant anecdote remained. He is to Louis as Castiglione is to Caravaggio, and Huet to Chardin.

The very real originality of the Le Nains can best be appreciated when we compare them with their Flemish masters. We can then see that their painting was a patient search for the essential, that is for humanity, and we can appreciate the sacrifice they made in discarding the 'quaint' themes of the pictures of their youth.

Flemish painting was a craftsman's tradition. Each painter had his own manner and his own repertory, which he handed on like a legacy or dowry. Succeeding generations swelled the inheritance with capital and interest. From 1525 to 1771, the Brueghel family to some extent possessed a monopoly of the *genre* scene, though it was contested by the Teniers clan until David Teniers the Younger married the daughter of Brueghel de Velours. Realism was the sole concern of the Flemish school, but it was ironic and ran to caricature. Burlesque treatment became a convention, false like every convention, and thus misleading. Its great vogue certainly cramped and falsified the conception of art for two centuries : Hogarth, Meissonier and Chocarne-Moreau were its inheritors. Brouwer's cynicism, his overt predilection for the vicious and lustful rabble was another formula. There was little place for observation and still less for psychology in such a limited art. What connection can there be between the 'bambocciatas' spoken of by Claudel, with their "dwarfs and goblins, cuffing, kicking, bawling out each other, in a welter of flushed faces, bloated paunches, which are all that Van Ostade and the Steens have to show us" and the sedate wisdom of Le Nain's peasantry? Yet all alike spoke for and portrayed the present; whether the present of Flanders, teeming with the future, or the present rooted in eternity of Descartes' France.

3

A NEW AWARENESS
OF TIME

THE WORLD OF REMBRANDT
THE PORTRAIT

T HE XVIIth *century brought to perfection that type of painting which best illustrates the humanist outlook : the portrait, and the human figure became the painter's proper study. Descartes'* famous Cogito, ergo sum, *the notion that man's presence in the universe suffices,* per se, *to give it a meaning, lies behind that pageantry of faces which from Velazquez to Van Dyck, from Philippe de Champaigne to Hals, is one long glorification of the human element. It was left to one of the greatest artists the world has known—to Rembrandt— to point out that man has his weaknesses besides his grandeur. Plumbing the depths of the human consciousness and deciphering the language of man's passions, he draws up, as it were, a balance sheet of the assets and liabilities, the sterling qualities and ineluctable defects, which leave their marks on each man's face. He calls in question all the traditional themes of painting, evocations of the sacred mysteries no less than portrayals of contemporary life; he infuses new life into the landscape, the nude, the still life, and enlists them in his unremitting quest of a new vision of reality. With a technique all his own, built of a vast store of accumulated knowledge yet ever enriched with new ideas that well up from the depths of his creative genius, he fashions a flesh-and-blood universe, at once vibrant with echoes of the past and an unfailing source of new discovery for future generations.*

THE WORLD OF REMBRANDT

The essential character of Rembrandt's originality lies in his way of using chiaroscuro and the powerful effect it produces inevitably governs the impression we retain of his work, that underworld of shadows and light peopled with biblical memories, contemporary moments and portraits of himself. Under its potent spell, we almost tend to forget how widespread a practice chiaroscuro was among XVIIth-century painters, though in Rembrandt's art it did not serve a simple, representational end, merely bringing out the fullness of volumes. Rather, with him, light-and-shade seemed to be the natural medium his temperament demanded, his imagination depended on. Rembrandt's creative genius appears to us now like a cosmic body whose whole course was a quest for balance among shifting elements, in promise now of light and favor, now of chaos and descent to darkness, a world of contradictions where blind forces ruled. When today we look back at the life he led, he strikes us as, at heart, an authentic Bohemian amid burghers, as unconscious of the morrow as of the past. His family, his pigment, his brush—these were his only measure of reality and, philosopher that he was, the hard facts of everyday had no existence for him. Even in his quiet years when it was plentiful, money was never more than a means to finer ends, the materials of his craft (and his searching often carried him far), the pictures of his private collection, his own home. The world he was building within stood in need of all he could bring forward. The material details of prosperity and poverty never deflected his singlemindedness. He knew what he wanted—though he was not sure how much of it was possible —and worked toward his goals with deliberate judgement.

His works are the statement of this outlook, indeed, this struggle. His chairoscuro, at times so overriding, is a weapon against the invasion of detail and extraneous factors. He bodied forth a vision of light, permanence and freedom, hewn from darkness by lines of force that play through the void, filling it with monumental life and scoring that world with a thousand unsuspected subtleties, as a lapidary does a diamond. His world is bounded by a wall of shadow—shadow that hides the unwanted and suggests the impending.

The fact is that, in the Holland of his day, the genesis of Rembrandt's world was the creative counterpart in art of historical events whose ultimate pattern no contemporary could divine, but which in time revealed the existence of a new world, almost before men suspected its presence. Their conscious efforts to build it had suggested, if not actually brought forth, conceptions whose essentially radical, futuristic spirit touched at many points the expressive nature of Rembrandt's art. Let us glance for a moment at these changes coming over XVIIth-century Europe.

While at Rome the Papacy was rebuilding the monarchy, and Paris and Madrid were falling into line with the new Catholicism, Protestantism was asserting an independence which was perforce accepted by a Europe powerless to crush it. Though, by the end of the XVIth century, Protestantism had lost some of its initial driving force,

Hendrickje as Bathsheba is painted life-size. This nude is perhaps closer to those of Tintoretto than to any other Italian nudes. But while in the Venetian's nudes we sense the yearning for a golden age that has left the world, Bathsheba, calmly seated among her draperies, weighs on them with a heaviness due less to the years than to a certain type of womanhood. She is neither goddess nor huntress, but "her whole form breathes the intimacy of everyday life, transposed into the calm regions and warm shadows of painting. Her flesh may hold a touch of weariness, but it has the warm bulk, the fullness of living matter and not of an artificially composed 'volume'." (Focillon)

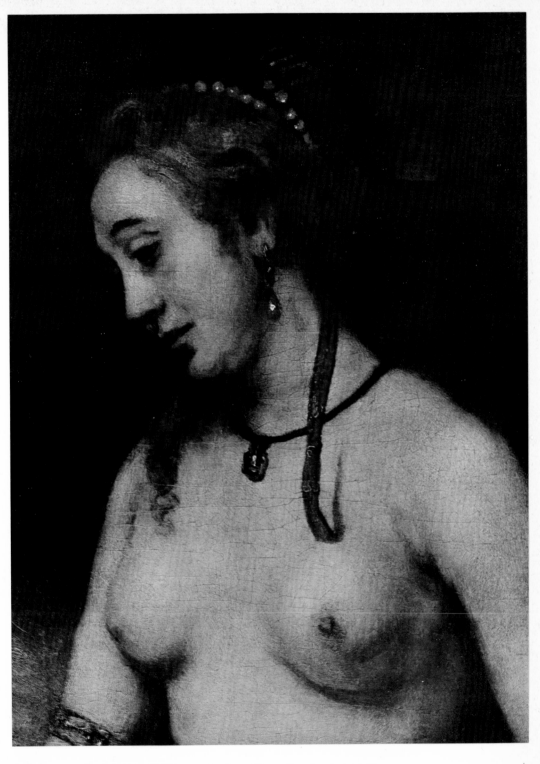

it had rocked the social, philosophic and spiritual foundations of the period. Ever since Luther launched his crusade at Wittenberg, religion had been harassed by anxieties which had not died down with the years. Luther's whole life was one long 'protest.' He aimed at establishing—and not only for himself—new relations between man and the universe and freeing the modern mind from the taboos and limitations whereby the Catholic clergy wished to prolong the Middle Ages *ad infinitum*. In demanding this freedom, Luther sponsored the authority and responsibility of the individual conscience as against the authority and responsibility of the Church, intermediary between God and man. This involved the establishment of a direct relationship between the Creator and his creature—a purely inner relationship, which meant that the spiritual life was no longer tied to the ritual of the Church.

REMBRANDT (1606-1669). CONSPIRACY OF CLAUDIUS CIVILIS, 1661. (77×121 ½″) NATIONAL MUSEUM, STOCKHOLM.

Led by Claudius Civilis, the Batavians swore an oath to revolt against the Romans, in the year 70 A.D., during the reign of the Emperor Vespasian. This theme, which symbolizes Dutch independence, was borrowed from Tacitus and chosen as the subject of a very large canvas commissioned from Rembrandt in 1660-1661 to decorate the gallery of the Amsterdam Town Hall. However, when it was hung, it failed to please the local magnates and was returned to the painter. It was not heard of again until the close of the XVIIIth century, when it reappeared, cut down to its present dimensions and was offered to the Stockholm Academy of Art in 1798. It was finally placed in the Museum in 1864. A drawing preserved in Munich shows the original composition : the table of the conspirators is set at the head of a long flight of steps in a large vaulted hall. On either side, there are secondary figures who serve as foils. Of the 25 square meters of this picture, only 6 square meters—the central part—remain. But this is enough to work the greatest fascination on all who see the work. For here Rembrandt has created one of those supernatural 'states' of light and shade of which he, alone of all painters, held the secret.

Thus there was a twofold revolution : first a spiritual revolution, from which man derived a new conception of himself and his relations with this world, criterion of his salvation or damnation ; and then the application of this inner liberation to the social structure. Throughout the XVIth century we see this new conception gaining ground irresistibly, while the ideology that opposed it underwent a gradual transformation in the course of the struggle. By the beginning of the XVIIth century, the new pattern had almost taken shape, although Germany, chief stronghold of Protestantism, was crushed by war and doomed to silence during two centuries of poverty and anarchy. Holland alone was able to counter the triumphs of Catholicism in Paris and Madrid, Vienna and Rome, with the forces of Protestant humanism.

It would be wrong to consider XVIIth-century Dutch society as being merely the expression of an essentially bourgeois way of life, over-much concerned with the preservation of material possessions. Holland had gained religious and political freedom at the expense of a long, heroic struggle which had left a permanent effect on the Dutch temperament. In this atmosphere of triumphant individualism, a remarkably orderly and

well-balanced social system was established. But behind this balanced structure, where even the smallest details were subjected to the discipline of the whole, man was still isolated, alone with his anxieties, inner doubts and dreams. And behind transparent façades mirrored in the shining peace of the canals, pioneers and sea-venturers were planning new departures. Rembrandt's career cannot be explained without reference to this dualism between the outer forms of life and the problems of the soul, which now were every man's personal affair. Others might portray the staid proportions of the Dutch interior, cosy still lifes and the

REMBRANDT (1606-1669). THE CONSPIRACY OF CLAUDIUS CIVILIS, 1661. DETAIL. NATIONAL MUSEUM, STOCKHOLM.

Such barbaric splendor, molded in light and colors of an oriental richness, is exceptional in Rembrandt's work. It is planned on a large scale and the technique is determined by the proposed location of the picture in the upper part of a banqueting-hall, where the light was poor.

Claudius Civilis is a figure of barbaric majesty and the indomitable energy of a chief assured of approaching victory. Roughed in beneath the curious, massive head-dress, the brutal face, distorted by the closed eyelid and almost buried under the beard and moustache, is fascinating in itself, and made even more so by the interplay of the many lines which cut the sloping blade—crossed swords and hands outstretched to take the oath. The rapid, emphatic brushwork brings out the flicker of the invisible torches illuminating the scene and stressing the curiously haunting face of the leader.

poetry of landscape, but Rembrandt was to plunge into the unconscious and explore the depths of racial memory.

Rembrandt, son of Van Rijn, a miller, was born at Leyden. There he had a sound classical schooling, but he left his studies to work with Jacob Swanenburch the painter, and, when he was eighteen, with Pieter Lastman in Amsterdam. Both Jacob and Pieter were convinced of the supremacy of Italy, where they had been trained. Though a fashionable portrait-painter of the day, Lastman, who had been Elsheimer's pupil, had none the less retained a taste for the exotic, for mysterious nocturnes treated at once meticulously and poetically. At twenty, Rembrandt had learned his craft and settled in Leyden. His first works were not unaffected by the realistic Dutch tradition, and showed his master's influence in their slightness and their color-scheme, a mixture of greys and browns with touches of bright color. But this limited manner proved too restricted for the young artist, who sought a wider field of inspiration in old drawings and engravings. In the Bible he discovered themes worthy of his genius, for he aspired to great and thought-provoking subjects treated on an epic scale. He waxed enthusiastic over any decorative element that might enable him to evoke the past or distant lands. A Turkish robe, a Persian sabre picked up in an Amsterdam shop, or a church vestment : each opened casements on that magic world of fantasy in which his proud and troubled spirit felt most at home. For such simple starting-points were enough to give his imagination wings. The subject was merely a pretext

REMBRANDT (1606-1669). THE CONSPIRACY OF CLAUDIUS CIVILIS, 1661. DETAIL.
NATIONAL MUSEUM, STOCKHOLM.

Out of the deep shadows emerge strange, masklike, sightless faces, built up with a lavish brush. As they are too far from the action to play any active part in it, the painter does not attempt to bring them into it and they are used simply for their fantastic effect, like Goya's nightmare creatures in the Deaf Man's House and Daumier's secondary characters. These faces, if exposed to the light of day, might be compared to the grimacing masks in Ensor's paintings.

REMBRANDT (1606-1669). THE FLAYED OX, 1655. (37×26″) LOUVRE, PARIS.

There has been much discussion as to the significance of this unusual still life in the work of an artist who rarely painted any, but "what gripped him in this *Flayed Ox* is neither a realistic ox, nor a glorified ox; it is his sudden sense of the immanence of a universe of which he feels this picture to be but one manifestation; it is as though in this scene of shambles a poignant symphony of form and color had found its perfect orchestration." (André Malraux.)

and, taking in his stride the limitations of time and place, Rembrandt attained complete plastic reality. Delacroix, later on, needed no more to conjure up the enchantments of the Arabian East, long before his trip to Morocco.

In Rembrandt's superb range of portraits, we should distinguish between those he painted on commission to pay for his bread and butter, and those he painted to please himself and indulge his inner demon. First of all, there is the gallery of notabilities, tedious, like all officials, in their social conformity and ill-concealed complacency; Rembrandt painted them accurately and with an almost irreverent insight. However, sympathy gained the upper hand whenever he sensed some physical or mental kinship with his model. And he shared in the spirit of inquiry of the great explorers, mathematicians and doctors of the age. Then there are the astonishing portraits of philosophers; for which it is attractive to think that Spinoza, Professor Tulp, and Jan Six, the collector, were his sitters. Sometimes he opened up his heart and depicted those he loved—Saskia, Titus, Hendrickje Stoffels—with wonderful tenderness and understanding. But his favorite and most rewarding subject was himself. He was fascinated by his own appearance and portrayed himself in turn as Grand Mogul, Ahasuerus, a philosopher, a great captain. Surely there could be no stranger Narcissus than Rembrandt as an old man in a turban with his staring, blotchy, withered face, great snufftaker's nose, soft, finely-drawn mouth and straggly beard, yet with an undiminished confidence in his own powers of seduction. Throughout his career, whether he was depicting handsome young men or disillusioned old ones, he constantly sought the reflection of his own personality—inquiring, self-complacent, proud and unsatisfied. This time, however, he was utterly sincere and made no effort to conceal the truth, for his arrogance was too thorough-going not to find an intense, masochistic pleasure in showing himself plunged in ever deeper ruin, yet with an ever fiercer pride.

Rembrandt considered that, in the smug, contented society in which he lived, the painter should act as an irritant. There have been many conjectures as to the exact significance of the *Night Watch* or, as it really should be called, *The Sortie of Captain Banning Cocq's Militia*. It has generally been considered as a hit at the traditional Dutch 'Corporation Pieces,' of which Frans Hals has given us such a delightful series. It is impos-

sible not to be struck by the cunning way in which Rembrandt has arranged his figures—one has an impression that they have been thrown into disorder by the intrusion of unexpected elements, most noteworthy of which is that seemingly irrelevant and quite inexplicable little girl with the cocks. The fact remains that this work, even assuming it has a satirical intent, has given the world a memorial, more enduring than brass, of what was doubtless no more than a commonplace institution.

Again, when he turned to the Bible, Rembrandt seemed invariably to select precisely such incidents as were best calculated to upset his orthodox brethren. With the curious result that the sacred world of his Old

REMBRANDT (1606-1669). OLD MAN ASLEEP, 1629. (20½ × 16″) SABAUDA GALLERY, TURIN.

Rembrandt painted this picture when he was twenty-three ; in it he has already succeeded in obtaining an exceptional intensity of light and shadow. Just as the *Conspiracy of Claudius Civilis* is not an historical painting, so this is not a portrait, but a meditation. One hardly sees the body, swathed in a light that seems to emanate from within. Thus, Rembrandt, who had scarcely emerged from adolescence, showed even at this stage of his career a fondness for silence and lonely places. The two *Philosophers* in the Louvre, dated 1633 and set in a warmer light, develop the theme of the recluse, in this case poring over texts in a queer room with an oddly dreamlike spiral staircase.

Testament paintings seems to be corrupted, stricken by some mysterious plague. All the sins of Israel—the worship of gold, debauchery, the thirst for forbidden knowledge—lurk in the very folds of the garments worn by his Davids and Judges. Here we surely have a vision older than Christianity; or is it the reprobate's monstrous predilection for the tainted? Nevertheless, the legendary East of antiquity comes vividly to life; the immemorial setting for the biblical drama is diversified with beggars from the local 'Street of Owls,' fantastic Rabbis and voluptuous Jewesses from the Amsterdam ghetto.

Rembrandt's originality lies not so much in his amazing inspiration as in the power of his expression, and he was the greatest psychologist in portraiture that the world has seen. For a long time his palette was skimpy, somber, almost monochrome; but golden russets and muted reds struck fire into these ashes, and beneath the gloomiest color-schemes can be glimpsed the etcher's urgent, compelling streaks of light. Behind the interplay of blacks and whites, there is a secret, throbbing life. The practiced hand of the graver gives the line a sharp graphic quality, distinctive as handwriting.

This, then, is the miracle of Rembrandt: there is not one of his works in which the technique is not as it were outstripped by the thought, yet not a single idea fails to find its appropriate means of expression, at once traditional and strangely new. In the mid-XVIIth century, Rembrandt revived the shadows of the Middle Ages, that 'corruption of the night' spoken of by Claudel, but from it he elicited young heroes and eternal truths. At the end of his life, when he was freed from all puritan and social conventions and his worldly hopes had foundered in disaster, he gave himself over completely to his dream. In resplendent purple and gold, he painted the *Denial of Peter*, *David and Saul* and *The Conspiracy of Claudius Civilis* with unparalleled magnificence.

Then, as Focillon puts it, "the West, which had reached the fullness of maturity was dazzled by an art, at once old and new, wrought of an eternal dream of man, the several powers of light and life and a heart's mysterious tenderness."

Rembrandt's pupils had his technique at their fingertips, but to reveal the mysteries of the human spirit, the divine spark is needed ; technique, however skillful, is not enough. Govaert Flinde, Aert van Gelder, Salomon Koninck and de Bray all painted in Rembrandt's manner but scaled down the master's message to their stature. Thus their works are far from being fulminant, awe-inspiring prophecies like Rembrandt's, and are more like the reassuring horoscopes supplied by fortune-tellers at a country fair. An exception was Carel Fabritius, the little painter of Delft, with his charming poetic sense ; if his work is but slight, it breathes sincerity. Indeed, his early death may well have deprived the century of a really great painter.

Rembrandt's genius was, in fact, too imperious, too absolute, for him to have many immediate successors. It is his most distant heirs— Goya, Daumier and Rouault —who approach him most nearly.

THE PORTRAIT

The Renaissance paved the way for humanism, and Leonardo gave it its program, which was exactly that summed up three centuries later in the famous line: "The proper study of mankind is man." Like the ode or epitaph, the portrait, more than any other branch of art, presupposes a host of conventions, and it tends to justify, or anyhow to explain, Mannerism. The seventeenth-century portraitists, even when carrying out an official order, refused to palter with their artistic conscience, they would have no truck with lies or even that pardonable lapse: idealization of the sitter. To fix the features of a face for all time calls for abnegation and humility; and this implies simplicity of style. The artist is not 'showing off' and he needs silence, so as to meditate and see to it that his testimony is that of an honest witness. The influx of humanism into Western culture could not fail to alter forms as well as values. The publication of Montaigne's *Essays* had not been in vain; the human mind and feelings whose prerogatives were finally determined in the seventeenth century were much concerned with the fact of man's nature and its corollary, his aspect. If the sense of Christian fellowship, that is of a communion of men, did not disappear, it had nevertheless suffered more blows than one since the Protestant crisis. The Reformation did not say "God is dead" but "God is elsewhere"—and consequently man as well. Descartes' first theorem began with the Ego and, while it is useless to speculate as to whether he would have turned atheist, had he lived in the twentieth century, it is certain that his own existence was intellectually more necessary to him than the existence of God. To free man was also to free his image. But this did not hold good everywhere. In Spain and Italy the portrait did not attain its independence, but expressed man the social entity, rather than man the individual. There were, however, other countries in which the reforming spirit had changed men's whole outlook on life. In Holland, first war and then political turmoil had enabled the reformed religion to survive. Reform implied a thorough-going revision of the foundations of religion and therefore of man. If France did not turn to Protestantism, it was primarily for political reasons, but also because she had sought her spiritual adventures in other fields. In other words, if the foundations of Catholic Christendom had not been destroyed, it was to the benefit of Catholicism, but to the detriment of Christ. For, in the seventeenth century, the great reformer and the real destructive force was no longer Luther, but Descartes. The references to God in the *Discours de la Méthode* treat Him merely as a stand-by, a convenient means of simplifying problems by shelving them, so as to concentrate the better on what he deemed the fundamental problem: namely man and the limitations of his powers. In fact, there is not a 'Christian' line in the whole book.

Velazquez approached painting with the ease that comes of conscious mastery. Neither the theme nor the representation interested him very much. Anything was welcome, provided it could come to vivid, dazzling life in a picture. Because he was Spanish, a Southerner, he was at first attracted by the life of the streets; afterwards, when he became a high official of the realm, it was on noblemen and kings that he bestowed immortality. He approached both types of subject with the same desire for exact interpretation. His image of man was what we see of him from outside, he did not try to penetrate the secrets of the heart. The thoughts of his model were those one normally assigned to him, his virtues those that his contemporaries extolled. This holds good even for his self-portraits. As a youth or as a figure in *Las Meninas*, he did not reveal any more of himself than could normally be perceived by his everyday acquaintances. With his other subjects, he made no attempt to interpret the individual; only to body forth the man before him at a certain moment of his life. Thus he painted, not Philip IV the man, but Philip IV, King of Spain, at eighteen and then at forty years of age. And the face does not swallow up the whole canvas, as so frequently occurred with Rembrandt, but is merely a component part of it. It is only a living object which happens to intervene between the background—landscape or interior—and the clothing, furniture or other inert matter in the picture. The focal point of the canvas is not the expression, which turns the picture into a portrait, but rather the model's sleeves or hat. All his faces seem to be gazing forth from the canvas towards the spectator, who might quite well join them there as part of the group portrayed, and this is true even of the group in *Las Meninas*: the Infanta, the jester, the painter, the maids—and the dog. Life here expresses nothing. Time is arrested and a splendid moment is held and captured—a moment in which beings with no personal destiny, no apparent past or future, are gathered together, mingling the charm of childhood with the tawdriness of the hirelings, the dullness of the setting with the splendor of the costumes. The color has faithfully seized a unique, well-chosen moment. Here we find neither sadness nor joy; only a wonderful orchestration of light and a riot of all-glorious color which suddenly lift the subject from the frame and give the participants a compelling human reality, but wholly lacking in emotion.

But Velazquez was not the only painter to have gone to Italy; Rubens, whose country was still under Austrian rule, halted in Venice and Bologna for some time. He was never to give the face that privileged position it was to hold in Holland. He had an obvious tendency towards 'presentation' in the theatrical sense. And this sense of the theater is manifest throughout his work, not only in the historical or mythological canvases, but also in his nudes. When he paints a naked woman, she has none of the secret yearnings, the vague regrets, whose presence we feel in Rembrandt's 'Bathsheba.' On the contrary, his nudes are forms of living, palpitating flesh, immediately desirable to all who see them, both within the canvas and outside it. The portrait of Helena Fourment and her children is a portrait of those who lived with him and gave him pleasure. Their goodness and their grace are the joy of his home life and he wants his friends, even casual visitors, to share his joy in them. There was a Southern side to his character—he was not a man to live at home in seclusion, but enjoyed meeting other people and mixing with them. Rubens' gallery contains portraits of men laden with honors and the civic virtues; there are fewer portraits of women than nudes, allegorical or real. If, at times, we feel that he has deliberately 'posed' their faces, this is not so much to express the

We have intentionally laid out these two charming portrait-groups facing one another. Curiously enough, despite the totally different worlds from which they come, the two groups of little girls, in pose and attitude, bear a striking resemblance to one another.

The little Spanish Infanta and her companion are decked out in ceremonial dress, the sumptuous costume of the royal court, and in them Velazquez' dazzling palette has found full scope for play. In so far as it is a portrait, we feel that the artist has sought to imbue her with an air apart, befitting her royalty, and further enhanced by the graceful, attentive deference of her companion.

In the portrait by Le Nain, the two little girls are peasant children. The attitude of the one on the right is much like that of the Infanta and, like her, she does not seem in the least distracted by the affectionate attention of her partner. Le Nain was by no means a master of Velazquez' stature. But he treats the clothing here with convincing simplicity and imparts to the faces a passive tenderness and air of wonder that are very touching. His tones give a sober lifelikeness to the subject and are perfectly suited to the simple truthfulness he sought to convey. The two pictures, so different in inspiration and technique, are closely linked by the warm human interest they hold for us.

None of Velazquez' many Infantas enjoys the celebrity of this picture. While the pictorial matter is heavy, the touch is light and the color brilliant. There is no story—a selected moment of life is glimpsed and held, and that is all. Here life has been disintegrated in terms of color.

"It is no easy task to define the subject of this picture. Is it a portrait of the Infanta Margarita with the maids-in-waiting and the royal household, or a portrait of Philip IV and his wife, or again a portrait of the artist himself engaged in painting this very work ? There was an old tradition that, in the center of the wall at the back, in portraits of this order, there should be a framed picture of the sitters' forbears so that deceased members of the family should participate in the family portrait. Here Velazquez keeps to this tradition, but gives it a new twist by presenting the reflection in a mirror of an older, but still living generation of the family.

"The severely geometrical lay-out, the frames of the paintings on the two walls, the frame of a mirror and the doorframe form a system of vertical and horizontal lines which determine the positions of the sitters' heads, so that what looks at first sight like a chance arrangement is really the result of careful planning in the artist's mind. There is a triple grading of the importance of the subjects in terms of the distance separating them from the spectator. Those in the foreground are the most fully modeled. They form a triangle in the bottom right-hand corner, a sort of frame and at the same time a foil ; those in the middle distance are handled more decoratively, while those in the background are shadowy. The light gradually diminishes from the center towards the margins of the canvas. The colors are subdued ; the pale harmony of silvery grey is broken only by a few patches of scarlet. At first sight, the artist seems to be only a subordinate figure in this court scene. Yet he is the only one who stands outside the rigidly hieratic group—the painter, the creator who can remake the visible world within himself." (C. de Tolnay) woman or man within as to lend greater immediacy to the sensuous effect. These faces do not invite us to explore the soul's inmost recesses, but simply to join them in the warmth and fullness of life as we all should like to live it, had we exuberance enough. This dramatic interpretation of the human face goes hand in hand with a vivid palette

and an overwrought treatment of gesture, tending to contrasts. Hence the heroic character of Rubens' portraits, a leaf he took from the book of the Venetians, and which led not only to a dramatic representation of faces and attitudes, but also to skillful arrangements of clothing and background. The framework of the portraits is a kind of brilliant, rapid sketch; the accents of the color give them life and it is in this respect that the Antwerp master has no peer. It was to him that Delacroix harked back, obsessed, as Rubens had been, by the problems of movement and colorful lifelikeness.

LOUIS LE NAIN (1593-1648). TWO YOUNG GIRLS, CA. 1630. (16¼ × 11¾") BOYMANS MUSEUM, ROTTERDAM.

The gorgeousness and sweep of Velazquez' art make a striking contrast to the humility of Louis Le Nain. While the Spaniard always magnified the subject, even if it was a common one, by the use of brilliant colors which swept away all trace of vulgarity, Louis Le Nain's models always retain the meagerness of tone and expression which the painter found in life itself. There is nothing fundamentally human about Velazquez' peasants. For him they never mean anything but charming pretexts for a picture. And his feat is all the more remarkable since usually it is the magnificent appearance of the subject that calls forth sumptuousness in the painting.

While the French portraitist, like his counterparts in Spain and France, can be regarded as performing a sort of priestly function vis-à-vis society, his duties as an artist differed considerably from theirs. Even if the seventeenth-century *honnête homme*—no negligible figure, since he was vouched for by Pascal and by Molière—played his part in external reality, his roots were in himself alone and his good sense was founded in eternity. In the face of conflicting passions, he stood for the calm assurance of a comprehensible universe in which he had his place. In his case, the portrait achieved full independence; it was not asked to 'tell a story' or to preach a sermon. To portray human reality was to create an image in which the wise authority of man, *homo sapiens*, shone forth. All the subjects belonged to the same type of humanity, one might almost say to the same class. Only Le Nain was able to find a world of feeling in the life of the people, but the very real greatness of his work was not to be appreciated until much later. Meanwhile portraits were character-studies and defined the type of man whose qualities had made the century what it was.

Although he came from Flanders, Philippe de Champaigne had an instinctive understanding of the French temperament. There was still something of the Baroque in him when he painted *Louis XIII crowned by Victory* and his Rubens-like allegories show his decorative side, but there is a much deeper truth in his numerous portraits of Cardinal Richelieu, where every trace of symbolism has disappeared. His portraiture, with its clean-cut outlines and suavity of color, is northern rather than southern in nature. Man and his triumphs are expressed in it with serene gravity. Using a sober range of color, the artist has applied himself, though less happily than Velazquez,

to supplying everything that could enhance and complete the portrait, particularly the clothes and the background. He never forgot that the face alone is not enough, but needs to be complemented by attitude and gesture,

PHILIPPE DE CHAMPAIGNE (1602-1674). MOTHER CATHERINE ARNAULD AND SISTER CATHERINE OF ST SUSANNA, 1662. (65×90″) LOUVRE, PARIS.

Philippe de Champaigne's daughter, a nun at Port-Royal, was miraculously cured of a long-standing illness after Mother Catherine Arnauld had made a novena for her recovery; this picture is an ex voto. The balance of the composition stems from the two juxtaposed right-angled triangles, with a vaguely indicated pyramid between, a shaft of light, the symbol of divine grace.

FRANS HALS (1580-1666). THE 'REGENTESSEN' OF THE HAARLEM ALMSHOUSE, 1664. (67×98″) FRANS HALS
MUSEUM, HAARLEM, HOLLAND.

As a poverty-stricken octogenarian, Hals was given assistance which saved him from destitution. In gratitude, he painted the *Regenten* and *Regentessen* of the local almshouse. In the treatment of the two canvases, we see intimations of his bitter struggle against adversity, but Hals was by no means a defeatist. The discreet red edge of the book on the table is a very modern way of enlivening the uniform expanse of black and white.

The faces and the hands have a touch of caricature. Claudel thus describes this picture. "If we screw up our courage to brave the scrutiny of this committee of five fearsome old ladies, we cannot but be aware of the livid stare of the six other semi-animate dummies placed behind us by some denizen of the netherworld. Neither in Goya, nor in El Greco, is there anything so masterly or so terrifying ; Hell itself has fewer horrors for us than this grim no-man's-land.... All accounts have been squared up, there is no more money left on the table ; only that firmly closed book, whose cover palely gleams like bone, and whose edge glows like hot embers. The first of the *Regentessen* at the corner of the table may strike us as the least alarming at first sight, but that sidelong look and her hands, one significantly open and the other closed, seem to say : 'That's all ! There's nothing left !' And the four other hags... ! But first of all, let us deal with the one who is bringing the President of the Committee a slip of paper which presumably bears our own name. We are facing a sort of female tribunal whose wimples and cuffs, isolating and stressing the mask-like faces and the hands, intensify the courtroom atmosphere. The tribunal sits, not before a crucifix, but before a picture showing the gloomy banks of a funereal river. Even if we can take our eyes off that skeleton-like hand, lying on the woman's knee, her harsh regard, tight lips—that book on which she leans tells us all we need to know ; we can expect no mercy from this good lady. As for the President, holding her gloves and fan in such a genteel way, her well-scrubbed face cleft by a hideous bird's-beak smile tells us that here we are dealing with something more implacable than justice—with nothingness. And how describe that miasmal sheen, the vampirish aura which emanates from these five figures, as from a decomposing corpse ?"

75

and he had an innate sense of composition, built up around the facial expression. The long hands and the symmetrical folds of the Cardinal's robe prolong the triangle of his face. Champaigne's fruitful contact with Jansenism should be stressed as yet another example of the influence of the new forms of thought on art. We must speak of Jansenism rather than Christianity here, for it was Jansenism that inspired that ascetic portrait of *Mother Arnauld* with its bare, uncompromising lines and the fine, withdrawn face, lost in prayer.

Because he was official painter to the King, Lebrun broke away but rarely from the decorative epic, the form of art most favored by the monarch and his circle. He was regarded by all his contemporaries as a very great master, and his work had real significance for them. It cannot be denied that he adapted his gift to the glorification of the monarchy and, if we shut ourselves to the circumstances of the period, his works seem cold and sterile. But he had breadth and, while his subjects were often so stylized as to be almost types, he drew the human face admirably. He was the originator of the court portrait, painted for a conservative society, whose liking for glory and nobility of mien called for decorative portraits and faces which, without actually being idealized, were only distantly concerned with realism. Mignard succeeded Lebrun in the royal favor. His Italian training was a hindrance and he could never quite free himself from the allegorical visions which had caught his fancy at Bologna. But if he lacked Lebrun's capacity for composition and decoration, his work as a portraitist is redeemed by his skill and his gifts as a colorist. Although Poussin found his portraits "frigid,

VAN DYCK (1599-1641). PORTRAIT OF AN ARTIST. DETAIL. REPRODUCED BY COURTESY OF THE TRUSTEES, THE NATIONAL GALLERY, LONDON.

Official portraitist of English high society, Van Dyck did his best to satisfy his sitters by giving them the artificial, mannered grace of the age. In this self-portrait we see the courtier and fashionable artist, but he also shows us something of himself, and that Rubensian rapture which too much etiquette has stifled. The narrow oval of the face, the unkempt hair, the keen yet anxious gaze, all tell of an unease, a touch of the Byronic 'spleen' of a later age. This slightly affected melancholy became in Gainsborough and Lawrence an elegant insouciance, apanage of an over-refined society.

artificial and without any ease or vigor," they are agreeable and even lifelike, when they are stripped of the mythological trappings in which he enveloped them and which were demanded by the period. Indeed the art of the last years of the century was vitiated by the practice of seeing the model from the aristocratic angle; the courtier had ousted the man, and the king replaced the social order. Skillfully as Mignard, Rigaud and Largillière competed with the decorator, lace-vendor and upholsterer, they went astray and lost their bearings on a canvas that was usually overcrowded; they stressed the startling detail and forgot the essentials. And the official portrait developed into a *genre* like the still life.

The Flemish painter Van Dyck worked at the English court, under the royal aegis. He was undoubtedly the most authentic of Rubens' disciples, but he added something of his own, namely a rakish elegance and a delicacy which combined to form the perfect means of expressing the life of seventeenth-century society. He had every gift, keen intelligence and an ability to give full expression to what he saw. For Rubens' epic grandeur, he substituted a subtler use of form. His aristocratic models gave him full scope for the employment of the most telling combinations of carefully chosen colors, and his portraits mirror the distinction, taste and elegance of the English court. To the tradition of Rubens, he added all that he had learnt from the Italians. He is an important figure in the history of painting, for he created a style which was undoubtedly the most delicate of his century.

Unlike Velazquez and Rigaud who basked in the royal favor, Frans Hals spent his whole life struggling against material hardships and long series of personal misfortunes. This should be stressed, for he must have had unusual strength of character not to have expressed the afflictions of his private life to a greater extent in his paintings. We have ample evidence of his struggles to keep the wolf from the door. He was married twice and had some dozen children who were a constant source of worry; one of them, half-wit, was brought up in an almshouse controlled by the Municipality of Haarlem. One of the daughters was relegated to the same almshouse at the age of fifteen to mend her evil ways. In the closing years of his life, Hals was so poor that the Municipality granted him three cartloads of turf every winter. And it was perhaps out of charity or a desire to combine a good turn with a good bargain that the Almshouse commissioned the *Regenten* and *Regentessen*. There is a last record of a payment of four florins 'for a tomb in the big church for Mr Frans Hals.' His paintings show the influences of the period, if not of his personal misfortunes, and in him we find the same directive current which inspired Caravaggio and traverses the work of Velazquez. But in addition to the realistic tendencies of the age he lived in, Hals had exceptional technical ability and, like Velazquez, was, first and foremost, a virtuoso. He worked hard and perfected a manner which he employed with great mastery. In his works we keep finding certain basic elements typical of the man himself: a simplicity of subject and representation, lucid execution and economy of means. Hals was a quick painter and his construction was sketchy, but always highly skillful. The light invariably came from only one side, the model was thrust into the foreground, and backgound reduced to a minimum.

Thanks to his realism, nourished by the living sources of the day, Hals never lapsed into the academic or the theatrical. He added a certain epic note to all his compositions without distorting the facts of visual experience. Much research has been devoted to his methods of composition and execution. Working with feverish haste, he flung drawing, colors, volumes and perspective simultaneously on the canvas. In his excellent book on Frans Hals, N. S. Trivas writes : "Hals represented light and shadow as a difference in color ; he painted objects by reproducing their color and design, that is to say, by distributing lights and shadows. Each stroke of the brush at once expressed volume, light, movement and texture. The colors are always pure and forthright. The black never tends to grey and the flesh tints have all their natural brightness. He never painted a thick black shadow near a luminous passage without using an intermediary shade." This excellent analysis of Hals' technique brings out clearly his affinities with the great modern colorists. As he grew older, he transformed his tones, changing his bright hues to greys, until black and white predominated almost completely. His style grew still more rapid and elliptic ; he called on the onlooker to add in his imagination whatever, in his haste, the painter had omitted. This sketchlike method has been recognized by the moderns as identical with theirs and they have acclaimed Frans Hals as a great master.

Rembrandt's subjects belong to another world. There is the order of the universe in which men feverishly seek to discover their place, and this is the order of Rembrandt. In a sense, Rembrandt was the only one of all these painters who did not belong to any accepted class or social organism. As a painter he stood alone, aloof—first of the 'outcast' artists. He did not depict individuals, but beings communing with spiritual presences—with Christ or Lucifer, laden with the immense burden of man's age-old questioning of that universe of which he forms an infinitesimal part. It is as though his aim were to interpret that image of man to which the spirit alone gives a meaning—that image which is sometimes lost in shadow, sometimes glorified by light, and perpetually wrapped in mystery. Such lofty solitude is not so easy to endure. In painting the *Night Watch*, Rembrandt made a break not only with Holland, but with all the anecdotal art in which Rubens, like Poussin, excelled. His was the far-ranging spirit of inquiry that goes beyond painting, and, for him, man was no longer anything but a focal point where universal destinies take shape through sufferings and perplexities and where mind and matter merge in the darkness of unknowing.

4
COLOR RHYTHMS
ARCHITECTURAL COMPOSITION

RUBENS · POUSSIN · CLAUDE

UNLIKE *Rembrandt, more and more a recluse as he grew older, Rubens always enjoyed mixing in all kinds of society. No art better than his voices the message of the Counter-Reformation in its hour of triumph, and in the huge decorations he made to the order of monarchs and religious authorities, he was the only painter of his day to carry on the traditions of the Italian Renaissance. But in his art, mythological and religious symbolism—spiced with typically Flemish sensuality—was put to the service of the present moment. His kings are gods, and his gods men; his color is pure poetry; his drawing, movement. Thus he applied a salutary antidote, rich in promise for the future, to the inert perfection of the over-compact, shut-in world of so many XVIIth-century painters. Poussin's counterblast to excessive individualism was no less salutary and lasting in its effects. For him, painting meant a tireless building-up of the world with elements on which he had reflected deeply; true, observation entered into it, but on the lowest grade of a hierarchy, at the top of which came reason and the feelings. Landscape, in his hands, became a sort of architecture, especially as he grew older (this holds good for Claude Lorrain, too), both truer and richer in significance and poetic overtones than nature herself. Calling as it did for an intense creative tension, Poussin's achievement sponsored a triumph of the intellect.*

THE POETRY OF RUBENS

The reaction started by the Carracci and Caravaggio against the enervating idealism of the Renaissance was carried on in Flanders by Rubens and in France by Poussin, if indeed the latter can be regarded as French, considering that so much of his life was spent in Rome. Rubens went to Italy in 1600 and stayed there for eight years. In that international center, he became aware of the universality of art. It must not be forgotten that, despite his admiration of Caravaggio, he also knew the decorations of the Carracci and learnt from them the secret of a universal and, indeed, European procedure, with which he tempered the more markedly indigenous qualities of his genius. In fact Rubens managed to combine two tendencies—Flemish and Caravaggesque realism and Italian idealism. Thus in his art we find a fusion of two ways of looking at the world, to the common gain of both. The fact that Rubens' tastes ranged beyond Caravaggio to Veronese, Correggio, Michelangelo and Titian, did not make of him an eclectic. And we would be wrong to apply the term 'Mannerism' to a form of humanism which reconciled the artistic heritage of the Renaissance with the message of the Church as defined by the Council of Trent.

Rubens was born in 1577. Tintoretto and Titian had just died and Veronese had not long to live. His teacher, Otto Vaenius, trained him to admire the Venetians, so it was natural that he should go to Venice (in 1600) to study them at first hand. When he was posted to Madrid as ambassador, it was again the Venetians and Titian that he found at the Escorial. He took all alike in his stride—the power of Michelangelo, Correggio's sensual grace and the composition of the Bolognese—though he was careful not to lose the joy in nature and all forms of life he had learnt from the Flemish primitives. And all these elements were transmuted in the crucible of his genius ; moreover he created new elements only distantly connected with these, indeed authentically his own. A humanist by upbringing, Rubens was very ready to combine the teachings of the past with the genius of his fellow-countrymen. He was the friend of Plantin and Moretus. His militant Catholicism (he was a zealous disciple of the Jesuits of Antwerp) drew him towards a more comprehensive, more contemporary view of art. The two components of Rubens' painting, both raised to their highest pitch by his soaring genius, make him the Baroque artist *par excellence*. None could be more Baroque than he, when he exalts his style to hymn the triumphs of the Church or 'spreads himself' to magnify the life impulse. All this rather rhetorical eloquence was a matter of temperament—and anyhow well-fed, prosperous Flanders never had a reputation for turning out ascetics—but it also illustrates an attitude which might be called Catholic, a certain indulgence to the weaknesses of the flesh and indeed an acceptance of all forms of life. But, moved by the deepest springs of his being, Rubens stemmed the anarchic urges of the life-instinct with the ritual formalism of the Counter-Reformation and the skilled technique of the Italian Renaissance.

In Flanders, essentially a land of craftsmen, in which each painter had his speciality and kept to it, Rubens was an exception. He tried his hand at everything and the world he created, his own, is universal. All was grist to his mill; he was too much of a painter to imagine that any form of life whatever, provided that it lent itself to plastic interpretation, should be excluded from his art. Life is not a system, and there is nothing less systematic than Rubens' achievement. He had no prejudices, no *parti pris*, and everything finds a place in his work: saints, martyrs, voluptuous nudes, apotheoses and Bacchanalia, mythological scenes and portraits, battles and landscapes. "He found release in creating worlds," Taine said, and Rubens himself, when he undertook the decoration of the great hall at the Luxembourg, declared: "To everyone his gift: my talent is such that I have never quailed before any task, however great the quantity and variety of the things to be portrayed." His copious, exuberant art is impossible to classify, and it is even more difficult to isolate any given work, for Rubens' world is a compact and homogeneous whole which defies analysis, and it is as a whole that it must be viewed. Yet Rubens invented nothing. The abundance and diversity of his inspiration seem to suggest a prolific imagination, yet nothing could be more traditional, nor more completely made up of humanist and Christian reminiscences. "I am infatuated with Antiquity," he said; but the miraculous feature of his genius was the modernity of his feeling for the past; for its interpretation in terms of the present. The Decius Mus cycle has the same contemporaneity as that of Marie de' Medici. Archaeology has no place in it; the allegorical content expresses an immediate psychological reality in timeless terms.

To clothe the immaterial in tangible form was almost a physical necessity for Rubens and not the least important feature of his naturalism. In this, he still belonged to the Venetian tradition, but his resolutely optimistic conception of nature was the delight of the healthy human being in his own powers. Though his heroes are confined in armor, their manly chests are well in evidence, their beards are thick and their virility unquestionable; the goddesses have small heads, but their hips are wide and suggestive of enormous fertility; even the martyrs suffer in the spirit of athletes bringing off some particularly arduous feat; and in all his figures the flesh quivers with seething vitality. Rubens was the only painter of his century who could really paint children, because childhood is a beginning and holds the promise of life. His old people, so different from Rembrandt's hypochondriacs, have kept the robustness of their prime, and he gives them a progeny like Abraham's. Rubens shut his eyes to the infirmities and blemishes of creation. Only obesity found any favor in his sight because it was a proof of superabundant health, as exemplified in Bacchus and Silenus. Health demands the light and warmth of the sun, and Rubens was certainly one of the 'happy children of Jupiter born in a fullness of light.' His models are given full prominence and the warm, glowing hue of their bodies ranges with their clothing and the background through that gamut of unbroken colors which he developed all through his career, from the luminous yellows of his Italian period to vermilion. Wherever the light falls directly on salient points, the flesh takes on a milky sheen: where the rays glance

RUBENS (1577-1640). CONQUEST OF TUNIS BY CHARLES V. UNDATED. (30×47″) BERLIN MUSEUM.

Nothing could be more typical of Rubens than this furious welter of men and beasts. Delacroix was to admire this impassioned lyricism and to give the same movement to his lion-hunts and battles between Greeks and Turks. But the smoke-laden sky reddened with the glow of battle reminds us even more of Turner. Charles V, seen on a bay horse to the left, is obviously taken directly from Titian's *Battle of Mühlberg*. Indeed in the figure of the Emperor we have an exact replica of the Venetian picture. In Tintoretto's Baroque figures (at St Mark's, Venice) we see a similar use of sweeping brushstrokes whose undulations closely follow the model's form.

across it, there are glints of pearly blue, a faint mist tinged with ultramarine. This tint grows fainter when the flesh is dusky; stronger, tending towards green or purple, when

it is pallid. Such a lavishness of 'Fauve' color must give an effect of sheer disorder, if it be not held in check by regularity of composition and an inner discipline. And at first sight, a work by Rubens gives the impression of complete confusion. It seems to have been dashed off in the heat of the moment; but this appearance is deceptive, for it is all subordinated to a deliberately concealed symmetry, an inspired arrangement of masses and values. Rubens had been careful not to forget what he had learnt from the Bolognese. The lay-out, perhaps unconscious in its origin, is necessary to emphasize the action, which is arranged in the form of concentric ripples fanning out across the canvas in fluent arabesques. What we find in Rubens is not the mathematically balanced lay-out of the Carracci but an inner rhythm, at once physical and psychological.

It would be a mistake to try to judge Rubens, the man, in terms of his art; indeed, however fascinating the man may be, he should really interest us only in virtue of his work. Nevertheless it is a paradox that such a gentle, unaggressive person, a born peacemaker, should have preferred the most emotional and violent subjects; that the happy lover of Helena Fourment, the exemplary family man, should have gone out of his way to find horrific themes; that the circumspect ambassador to Philip IV, Charles I and the Prince of Orange should have made no secret of his taste for scenes combining

RUBENS (1577-1640). THE CAPTURE OF PARIS BY HENRY IV, CA. 1628-1631. (9½ × 17½") BERLIN MUSEUM.

This is a sketch for one of the scenes from Henry IV's life commissioned by Marie de' Medici for the Luxembourg Palace. Here Rubens succeeds in combining Baroque lyricism with the stagecraft of the Venetians. But the striking thing about this picture is its colorful atmosphere, the interplay of warm browns and metallic blues—dark tonalities which, in a work by the Antwerp Master, come as something of a surprise.

the utmost refinements of sensuality with outrageous sexuality; and that a pupil of the Jesuits and their official painter, a good Christian and devout communicant, should have sought inspiration in mythology and pagan pantheism. To imagine that Rubens used his painting as an outlet for secret and repressed passions would be attributing to him a romantic character quite out of keeping with what we know of him. The truth is that all his pictures are pure conventions, excuses for painting and pretexts for rhetoric; for in Rubens there was much of the orator. His lyricism, the 'Pindarism' spoken of by Fromentin, demanded striking effects. His art was akin to that of the preacher and his preaching was of the kind that goes with much noisy ranting and flapping of lawn sleeves.

Unfortunately, it was the rhetorical side of Rubens' art that was copied by his disciples. Genius cannot be transmitted, but certain tricks of the trade were particularly

RUBENS (1577-1640). THE KERMESSE, 1635-1638. DETAIL. LOUVRE, PARIS.

This painting, which belongs to Rubens' final period, sums up and symbolizes his whole career. It is a Saturnalia of people who seem to have sprung from the earth and partake in its fertility. This work had an immense influence on XVIIIth-century French painting. Watteau, who copied it in 1709, often drew inspiration from it, adapting its hectic, frenzied gaiety to his elegant, gallant manner.

RUBENS (1577-1640). PORTRAIT
OF HELENA FOURMENT WITH HER
CHILDREN, 1635. (44 ½ × 32 ½")
LOUVRE, PARIS.

During the closing years of Rubens'
life his amazing genius went from
strength to strength. He retired
with his young wife and children to
a country manor, furnished to his
taste. Tired of society life and more
and more wrapped up in his art, he
turned to works in which decoration
was no longer his chief concern and
he could express his personal responses without regard to the preferences of his buyers or the powers-
that-be. This picture is both a
record and an illustration—an illustration of happy family life, of a tender yet warmly sensual affection,
gladdened by Helena's extreme youth
and Rubens' pleasure in his healthy
children. It is also an example of the
painter's procedure. First the principal values were laid in upon a uniformly golden-brown background.
Then he picked out the drapery and
the child's hat with touches of red.
Finally he added lighter tones to all
the faces to emphasize the glow of
the flesh, and particularly to the neck
and half-bared breast, so that the
color seems to carry on the movement.

easy to learn from Rubens,
since he made his disciples
follow his own technique as
far as possible, so that when
he had paintings on the
stocks they could complete
them. For his studio was
nothing short of a picture-
factory; and to keep up
the output his pupils had
to conform strictly to their
employer's instructions.
Actually this seeming high-
handedness opened the way
to modern painting. Van
Dyck and, through him,
the subsequent course of
English painting can be
traced back to Rubens.
XVIIIth-century French

RUBENS (1577-1640). ABRAHAM'S SACRIFICE, CA. 1620. (19½×25½")
LOUVRE, PARIS.

Here the influence of the Venetians can be clearly seen. Quite obviously Tintoretto suggested to Rubens the spiral movement which carries the eyes along the diagonal recessions of the composition. Titian treated the same theme with the same violent foreshortenings and the same swirling movement, fusing flesh and sky in one tremendous blaze of light. But to Rubens himself belongs the frenzied violence of the coloring, the maelstrom of forms, the vigorous lay-out and its brilliant illusionist realism.

painting learnt its idiom from the Luxembourg Gallery. Watteau, Gros, Delacroix—who was full of enthusiasm for the Antwerp triptych and even dreamed of being another Rubens—Renoir and Matisse went to school with Rubens.

But such illustrious descendants should not make us forget his many humble heirs among the Flemish artists of the XVIIth century. There was Crayer, for instance, of whom Gillet said: "Nobody spoke the bold, florid, worldly-cum-ecclesiastical language

of Baroque as he did." Jordaens was the Caravaggio of Flanders. He developed inde-
pendently of Rubens, but was confirmed in his full-blooded naturalism by Rubens'
precedent. Van Dyck achieved a position which he would doubtless not have deserved,
had Rubens not inspired him.

RUBENS (1577-1640). THE FATES SPINNING THE DESTINY OF MARIE DE' MEDICI, 1622.
LOUVRE, PARIS.

Rubens' work as a decorator and official court painter was considerable, and he was commissioned by Marie de'
Medici to decorate the big rooms at the Luxembourg. Here the composition is broadly conceived, while the inspiration is
typical of the Renaissance. Yet, in spite of the Italian influences, the allegorical nudes are uncompromisingly Flemish.

POUSSIN · CLAUDE LORRAIN

At the opposite extreme to Rubens' tumultuous dynamism and Baroque restlessness, stands Poussin's classicism, an approach to art of a very special order and the product of formal theories adhered to with remarkable tenacity. Who was Poussin the man? Perhaps, by dint of so much analysis and self-discipline, he hardly knew himself. A painter cannot identify himself with an abstract and would-be universal doctrine without making great sacrifices. And it is these sacrifices rather than the extent to which he achieved his ideal that make us like or dislike Poussin.

Every generation of French painters has subscribed to an artistic theory. Each group, each school, if not each painter, has evolved an aesthetic ideal and published it in the form of a treatise or manifesto. That their works do not always fit in with the program they have set themselves is immaterial. Every generation has claimed to possess not necessarily talent, but the secret of artistic truth and, in the light of its own tenets, has condemned the mistakes of previous generations. Poussin took up the cudgels, as boldly and ardently as Delacroix at a later date, in order to free painting from that vapid affectation which was the aftermath of the Renaissance, and much credit is due to him for this. And this seemingly negative achievement had its positive side. Once the taint of sentimentality and the trivial had been eliminated, his next problem was to arrive at a form of painting which, purified of extraneous and incidental features, was disciplined and permanent, reflecting the classical conception of man. "The senses disintegrate, the mind integrates," as Braque was to say. Pure painting is a contradiction in terms if this is taken to mean that the purely pictorial element in a painting can be isolated. Descartes said that weight is the dimension of falling bodies and in the same way painting is the dimension in terms of which the painter sees and interprets an object. The aspiration of the French towards pure painting (which ultimately led to Cubism and Abstraction) is surely not a desire to strip the picture of all but its aesthetic content, which would be inconceivable and absurd, but to treat the whole of its content in a painterly way. In the seventeenth century the senses which enable us to apprehend the external world were subordinated to the understanding. *Cogito, ergo sum*, said Descartes, and Malebranche observed: "Thought alone is the specific essence of the mind and the various ways of thinking, like those of feeling and imagining, are but the modifications of which it is capable and by which it is not always modified." Pure painting should therefore embody pure mind and express pure thought. Poussin wrote in his *Observations*: "Painting is nothing else than a visual concept of spiritual things, and in showing material objects, it represents solely the order and nature of those things."

We should like to bypass theories and deal simply with the painter, who after all is more important from our point of view, but there is so much calculation and deliberation in Poussin's premeditated art that his thought must be understood before we can gain an adequate idea of him. He also said: "Beauty does not emerge in a work of art unless it is prepared for as carefully as possible beforehand. Such preparation consists in three things : order, manner and true specific form." This was one of his famous Precepts. But such systematic thought in a painter is artistic suicide. The academicism which sees that doctrine is respected leads nowhere; it is a mere subject of discussion amongst aesthetes. Poussin's instinct must have been stronger than his ideas for him to have survived when Lebrun and so many others went under. "The miracle,"

POUSSIN (1594-1669). THE TRIUMPH OF NEPTUNE AND AMPHITRITE, 1638-1640. (44¾×57½")
MUSEUM OF ART, PHILADELPHIA.

This canvas was commissioned to decorate Richelieu's castle. The allegorical and mythological inspiration is identical with Raphael's in the same scene at the Farnesina. There is a Baroque gusto about the composition, rather unexpected in Poussin, but disciplined by the arabesque formed by the figures and their grouping, still very much in the Bolognese manner.

This picture, together with *Winter, or the Flood*, *Spring, or the Earthly Paradise* and *Autumn, or the Grapes of the Promised Land*, was commissioned by Richelieu. This sequence of the Seasons was painted between 1660 and 1664. Poussin could not conceive of nature except in terms of the antique. To paint *Summer*, he required a biblical subject. He strove here to reconcile Raphael's order with the disorder of the Venetians, in which harmony is sacrificed to expression. But Poussin remains a painter in whom "freedom of expression is not impaired by any fixed manner of execution."

SO MUCH THEORY IT IMPEDED HIM

observed André Gide, "is that Poussin's greatness was such that, in his case, the vessel did not burst under the pressure of its contents and his thought succeeded in subduing his material while at the same time exalting it. This is because in him thought immediately became image, it was born in plastic form, and purpose, emotion, form and craftsmanship fused within him to create the work of art."

The prestige of Rome as an art center at the beginning of the XVIIth century was upheld by the illustrious pupils of the Carracci and Caravaggio's successors, and can be estimated by the number of French painters who undertook the long journey to Rome, many of them settling there for good. The pilgrimage to Italy had become so much of a tradition that Le Sueur, who had not been to Rome, was long to lament this gap in his education. Domenichino, Guido Reni and Lanfranc trained decorators, and such masters of perspective as Zoccolini taught pupils how to solve the problems raised by arches and cupolas—for France was in need of decorators. The second school of Fontainebleau had, as it were, died of sheer inanition and in 1617 Marie de' Medici had had to call in Rubens to decorate the Luxembourg Gallery. Vouet's success on his return from Rome in 1627 was assured not only by his merits, but also by the large number of commissions he received from the King, the Cardinal, the nobility and the clergy. Brought up on Raphael, the Carracci and the Venetians and influenced by Caravaggio in Rome, Vouet was

POUSSIN (1594-1669). SUMMER, OR RUTH AND BOAZ, 1660-1664. DETAIL. LOUVRE, PARIS.

In spite of the biblical subject, Poussin frankly yielded to the seduction of the voices of the earth in this picture. Here all things breathe his love of nature, refined by thought. Forms and planes harmonize perfectly with the color to hymn the enchantments of this Virgilian landscape shimmering in the heat. It reminds us of Corot's Italian landscapes.

generously gifted, capable of pleasing invention, skillful in ornament and able in execution. As he had so many commissions to cope with, young painters flocked to his studio to work along with him. Blanchard and Claude Vignon went to Rome in 1623 and 1628 respectively, but were doubtless more attracted by Venice. François Perrier, famous for his decorations at the Hôtel La Vrillière, was one of Lanfranc's pupils. Valentin, a protégé of Urban VIII, stayed in Rome where he adopted Caravaggio's realism. Stellard de Lyon, Pierre Mignard and Dufresnoy were convinced that only the Eternal City could produce true painting. Errard, who settled in Rome shortly after 1620, became so Roman that he was appointed Director of the Academy of France on its foundation. Sébastien Bourdon, who arrived in 1630, had a sort of genius for pastiche and imitated the 'Bambocciatas' of the many Flemish painters with whom he consorted. All these French painters came to Rome to hammer out the personal style that each aspired to, under the guidance of the masters. Only one—in this respect the least French of them all—succeeded both in absorbing the Roman precedents and in enriching his own genius : Nicolas Poussin.

Poussin was born in 1594 at Les Andelys. His Norman origin, which he indicates with such obvious pleasure in the self-portrait dedicated to Chantelou, seemed to him to be the most authentic part of his debt to France. Certainly, on that occasion, he did not attempt to claim any kinship with his fellow-countryman Corneille, whose virile poetry and epic sweep were compassed in as strict a form as his own compositions, but rather to evoke his first childish enchantment with nature, the source to which he was constantly to return. Félibien does not say where or how Poussin acquired his wide Latin learning, and his early days are shrouded in almost complete mystery. Of those essential first thirty years we know next to nothing, despite research and a host of more or less fantastic theories. What little we do know and a few scattered dates are not enough to enable us to form any final opinion on his training. This much, however, is known : that he was made aware of his vocation by Quentin Varin, who came to paint altarpieces at Les Andelys and that, at the age of eighteen, he followed the painter to Paris. The Marcantonio engravings, after Raphael, which he saw at the home of Courtois the mathematician were a revelation to him. Twice he attempted the journey to Rome and twice he failed. He encountered great hardships, did odd jobs in the provinces and at the Luxembourg, and there the goldsmiths' guild commissioned him to paint a 'May' for Notre-Dame. Cavalier Marin, impressed by his abilities, urged him to make the journey to Rome, and he left Paris, without regret, at the beginning of 1624. In Rome he was eager to learn all he could and set to studying the masters, particularly Titian. "A painter becomes skillful by observing things rather than by tiring himself out copying them." He took notes, drew, and observed nature. But he was not content to learn about things through the senses or through the medium of the greatest painters. According to Félibien, he sought to discover the reasons for the different kinds of beauty to be found in works of art, since he was convinced that a craftsman could not attain the perfection he aspired to without first charting the paths leading to it and the pitfalls on the way. In his own eyes, his greatest fault was probably his temperament—his instinctive approach to painting. He treated it as a weakness, reproached himself with it as with a sin, and subjected himself to severe discipline. Alberti's treatise was his Bible, geometry was his guide, and reason his never-failing arbiter. "There are two ways of seeing an object," he said, "one is simply to see it and the other is to examine it closely. When we see simply, the eye receives the form and appearance of the object in question, but when we examine an object closely, we seek to know it thoroughly through patient observation, in addition to the simple and natural reception of its form by the eye. Thus it can be said that simple seeing is a natural operation and that what I call the 'prospect' is an operation of the thinking mind." What he sought to discover was the essential truth which remains unaltered beneath the diversity of appearances. It was his habit to draw from memory, referring only to jottings in his sketchbooks. Working from memory rather than nature was his way of getting what he called "the prospect."

This tendency towards abstraction isolated him from his *milieu*. Caravaggio horrified him so much that he believed that he had come into the world to destroy painting, just as the pundits of the Salon thought that Cézanne was "the greatest criminal of modern times." He shared the admiration of the Carracci's pupils for Raphael, but his natural caution and intellectual bias instinctively put him on his guard against their grandiloquence and facility. He considered Domenichino's *fa presto* as a betrayal of the intellect. "The painter's hand should not produce a single line which has not previously been conceived in his mind." Such conscientious calculation enabled him to achieve his self-imposed aim : "The imitation in lines and colors over a certain area of everything that can be seen under the sun," though he added a corrective, which must be stressed as it is too often forgotten : "Its purpose is to give pleasure."

Now let us consider how Poussin arranged his subjects, which he took from the vast repertory of mythology, with a preference for those that were noblest and had most appeal for the intellect. After determining what parts should be included in the composition and arrangement of the picture, he eliminated those he considered irrelevant and confusing, and stressed the principal figures by subordinating the secondary ones, giving each its proper place and assigning to it its appropriate action. Thus every element of the picture contributed to the perfection of the lay-out. Next, he concentrated on beauty rather than adornment, which had to be simple and in conformity with the subject. Laid out as an arabesque, the composition obeyed an abstract rhythm. Poussin was certainly haunted by the idea of movement, but his secret, half-unconscious ardor was held in check by his sense of proportion, which immobilized the composition by means of lines intersecting at right-angles ; it is as though he felt obliged firmly to curb every impulse that might deflect his aim. Such systematic insistence on the right-angle is only possible in frontal compositions, but the painter added diagonals which almost imperceptibly direct the perspective and suggest recession. The horizontal and vertical features, often laid out according to the *Golden Section*, are balanced as harmoniously as the bays in architecture. Moreover, the buildings which he introduces, as much for their straight lines as for their antique character, set the standard. This sort of landscape

POUSSIN (1594-1669). ORPHEUS AND EURYDICE, 1659. (49×88 ½″) LOUVRE, PARIS.

In contrast to Claude's vision of nature, already half way to Impressionism, nature as Poussin saw her did not dare to be simply landscape, but preened herself in mythological trappings. The static figures are balanced by the architectural arrangement of the trees, the full volumes of the hills, castle and clouds, and the intense color, which is not unlike Cézanne's.

owes nothing to Giorgione or Titian, but stems from the strict, logical landscape of Bellini, whose *Banquet of the Gods* Poussin copied.

This constant bridling of emotion—"the Rule that corrects emotion" as Braque put it—also succeeds in checking our appreciation. For us, a picture should have emotional significance and should be something more than an intellectual puzzle. We cannot share Lebrun's enthusiasm for those riddles worthy of the casuists which Pascal held up to derision in his comments on the *Carrying-off of St Paul*. "The three angels carrying St Paul represent the three states of grace : the first being the effect of that grace which theologians call prevenient and efficacious, the second the effect of conco- mitant or helpful grace, which is not so striking as the first, the third the perfect and constant state of abundant and triumphant grace which accompanies the elect in this life ... The leg of the Saint which points downwards represents his self-confessed leaning towards sin ... the angel's hand supporting the leg represents the support he receives from grace"—and so forth. Such labored mixtures of naïvety and pedantry were nevertheless greatly admired by contemporaries. If Poussin's merit lay only in such intellectual exercises, his work would now be just another curious example of XVIIth-century thought ; but the prim, set mask of the pedant concealed a colorist gifted with a sensibility always struggling to assert itself. It has too often been forgotten, as P. du Colombier observed, that while he had the same love for beautiful women as for beautiful pillars, he also had the same love for beautiful pillars as for beautiful women ; that the

CLAUDE (1600-1682). LANDSCAPE WITH MILL, OR WEDDING OF ISAAC AND REBECCA, 1648. (59½×91½")
REPRODUCED BY COURTESY OF THE TRUSTEES, THE NATIONAL GALLERY, LONDON.

No artist has ever depicted the depth and distance of a landscape or the delicacy of a horizon so happily as Claude. He was principally interested in the play or reflection of light on water, or its dispersion through a cloudy sky. His pictures do not have the clarity of the Roman landscape or the trees of Italy. The light mists and background lost in the distance are already in the French manner, as is the light filtering through the trees and the dense leafage, this very special rendering of which was, later, to be Watteau's.

figures of his Bacchanalia are swept along by dancing rhythms and that, in his great landscapes, the alliance between sky, trees and water and majestic scenes of history and mythology, implement a feat unparalleled in the history of painting—a feat whose secret he had not learnt from the Carracci and which was the despair of all those who tried to imitate it.

Thus it was in landscape, devoid of invention or archaeological and scholastic significance, that Poussin dared at last to be himself. And now it was the Roman landscape, and not any categorical imperative of doubtful value, that imposed its discipline on the painter. Poussin happily yielded to the rhythms of nature. He ceased to reason and indulged to his heart's content in the bliss of the Golden Age that he rediscovered in this Virgilian landscape, where the myths of old blossomed into new life. Like Corot, he expressed directly and effortlessly the poetry of a countryside which breathes eternity. Thus, by a roundabout way, Poussin, who had for so long been a conscience without morality, a psychologist without psychology, finally lit on the underlying poetry of his art, this perfect harmony between man and nature, which he never referred to in his theories. Was this heedlessness or the dream of the exile who, through the medium of the Roman landscape, recalled the far horizons of his Norman homeland ?

This new tendency, which began in 1645, grew increasingly pronounced during the remainder of Poussin's life. The figures become less and less important, while the landscape becomes the very expression of the painter's thought and acquires a sensitive poetic quality: a commentary on the theme which is barely indicated, just as an orchestra takes up and embellishes a solo theme. The *Landscape with Three Monks*, where an unruffled, lonely lake suggests the hermit's placid existence, is particularly striking in this respect. The subject is slight—three monks in conversation—but the gloomy expanse of water, cut off from the world by a barrier of rocks topped with distant dwellings, imparts an atmosphere of meditative silence, congenial to the theme.

This canvas is not an isolated case ; in the Louvre *Diogenes* of 1648, the theme of the philosopher throwing away his bowl on seeing a shepherd drinking from the hollow of his hand, is again no more than an excuse for the building up of an austere landscape, whose nobility and severity are an appropriate setting for the philosopher's discovery. The *Funeral of Phocion* dates from the same year, but its strict geometrical construction, its host of little characters and the importance of the architectural features show that Poussin was reverting to his more intellectual viewpoint after a brief respite.

In Rome, in the same year, Claude Lorrain, his junior by six years, painted two works which are particularly significant when set beside those of Poussin. They are the *Wedding of Isaac and Rebecca* at the National Gallery and the *Embarkation of the Queen of Sheba* at the Louvre. In these we see the work of a painter who has fully mastered his means of expression. At no other moment can the divergent paths of the two painters have been closer. Let us consider, for a moment, why this was so. Claude's method at the outset was the same as Poussin's, and he closely studied nature. "Eager to penetrate the secrets of art and the mysteries of nature, Claude rose at dawn and stayed out of doors until nightfall, so as to mark all the subtle changes of the twilight hours and render them exactly.'' Sandrart, who has just been quoted, saw Poussin working in the country and making his nature sketches, which are so close to Claude's that sometimes even connoisseurs find it hard to be sure to whom they should be attributed, the main difference being that Poussin's sketches are in strongly contrasted washes, while Claude's are less clearly defined, though both are equally obsessed with light.

Although their aims are similar, their efforts diverged once they reached the studio. Poussin, as we have seen, was not content with mere appearance and painted a nature almost more real than the reality. The features he gave it were taken from the real world and stones, bushes and trees all have their specific characteristics; the birch is distinguished from the laurel, the pine from the poplar. Nevertheless they are so many components arranged in a certain, preconceived order. The geometrical balance of his composition was, in the last analysis, directed by the artist's mind exclusively, and thus the heroic landscape was born. Claude was inspired by the same nature, bathed in the same light, but he was not so ambitious. His powers of invention proceeded from his sensitivity and imagination. In nature he sought the luminous rather than the rational equivalent. His simple soul asked no more than to succeed in portraying the harmony of the Roman landscape bathed in a sunlit atmosphere. In Claude's paintings there is the naïvety of a Douanier Rousseau. Among his contemporaries he was not regarded as an expert artist and the subordinate duties he had to perform for Agostino Tassi, his master, were cited to excuse his lack of learning. He was called ''an inspired idiot,'' but credit had to be given him for his knowledge of aerial perspective and the nuances of atmosphere, even if he knew nothing about linear geometry. What matters to us is that he was the first to capture light in a picture, to represent the sun directly, to touch the crest of every wave with vagrant gleams and to bathe his countryside and woodlands in a soft, dreamy twilight. In short, it was by his exquisite portrayal of light as much as by his Arcadian poetry that Claude breathed new life into the language of his predecessors.

Sandrart's rather summary biography makes us wonder whether Claude and Poussin ever came in contact with each other. There does not seem to be any evidence for it, but it is even less probable that they were unaware of each other's existence. It was not by chance that Poussin started his historical landscapes about 1645 when Claude's were very much in vogue. The circumstance that after the brief, strongly contrasted 'jottings' of his early work, he gave more brightness to his skies and their nuances surely owes something to Claude. And, on the other hand, the way in which Claude's rustic subjects were succeeded by historical paintings—*The Village Dance* by *The Wedding of Isaac and Rebecca*—suggests a desire to vie with Poussin.

Claude's strength lay in his portrayal of the sky no longer as a curtain, but as having depth and vast recession. The Flemish painters had started the landscape and Patinir had excelled in it. The Northern traditions had been introduced in Rome by Paul Bril, from whom Agostino Tassi learnt them. But Claude, with the superb indifference of the self-taught artist, changed everything and bodied forth his own vision ;

Patel in France and Berchem in Italy did not attempt to hide their debt to him. His practice of enclosing his gold-glittering air between the pillars of a temple or among ships, "moored by an anchor of desire and dreams," was discarded by the Impressionists when they tackled the same problem. They imagined that they had solved it, yet what work by Monet attains the luminous intensity of a Claude? Only Van Gogh with his boldness and swirling brushwork was able to equal him in rendering the noonday sun. Let us, for a moment, imagine the landfall of those ships bound for the Land of Spices or the Island of Cytherea. Goethe was well aware of the unreal side of these fabulous departures. "They (these pictures) have the greatest truth without the slightest shadow of reality." Claude Lorrain knew nature by heart down to its smallest details and used it as a means of expressing a world whose soul was purest beauty. His was the true idealism; he could use real means in such a way that the true, when it emerges in his work, has the semblance of absolute reality.

This is not a French conception, if by this we mean a desire for the logical, intelligible, universal order preconized by Poussin. In any case it is an anachronism and more akin to late XVIIIth-century English Romanticism than to the spirit of its own period. In spite of his success, Claude had no immediate influence in France. He was an isolated figure, taken to England's heart long before Turner's revelation of him. And it was due to his being associated with the English landscape-painters that Claude was finally repatriated and begot his unfilial offspring, the Impressionists, who refused to acknowledge his paternity.

5

THE ORDERING OF SPACE

OBJECT AND THE LANDSCAPE
VERMEER AND THE PLAY OF LIGHT

IT IS *a far cry indeed from Caravaggio's still life, the basket of fruit placed well in the foreground, in empty space, to those Spanish 'bodegons' in which Zurbaran and Velazquez began by placing isolated objects with as yet no link between them, yet which were already beginning to come alive, each developing a curious internal warmth. Gradually these elements fall into place, join in building complex compositions, and come to be located in recessive space. And, even when they form part of a wider subject, they are no longer minor elements but play an active part in it. Thus a sort of dialogue arises between the inanimate objects and the personages, a dialogue which reaches its perfection in Vermeer's art. Objects and figures participate in the same life, a life instilled by the light that hovers and is reflected upon them. The source of this light seems to lie within the picture itself, and it moves freely amongst the figures and objects, bringing out their volumes. These exquisite forms are arranged in a most skillful manner, which, emancipating them from any accidental or merely picturesque significance, has something of the harmonious elegance of a law of geometry. And depth is suggested by the angle of the walls, by doorways, by the arrangement of the furniture. This method is also applied, and with wonderful success, to the lay-out of the Dutch towns and landscapes. The new science of optics enabled the painter to penetrate to the heart of the mystery. And in the vastness of the skies he retrieved the notion of infinity.*

THE STILL LIFE

While the triumphs of Catholicism in Antwerp, Madrid and Paris inspired or compelled artists to glorify the Divine or, with somewhat less conviction, the heroic deeds by which the potentates of the day had won their high place in God's universe,

EVARISTO BASCHENIS (1607 OR 1617-1677). MUSICAL INSTRUMENTS. DATE UNKNOWN. MUSEUM, BERGAMO.

Baschenis made his reputation with still lifes of musical instruments in the violin-making towns of Bergamo and Cremona. Here the instruments have fallen silent but the canvas still vibrates with echoes. The perfection of these forms and their coloring gives them the look of gorgeous butterflies or beetles arranged by the hand of a master-architect.

FRANCISCO ZURBARAN (1598-1664). STILL LIFE. (33×18″) PRADO, MADRID.

Instead of grouping his objects in a studied arrangement, Zurbaran applies himself to scattering them, but he redresses this seeming negligence by the color which binds them together. The various effects are balanced, colors are skillfully played off against each other ; here, the harmonious and mathematical relationships are infinite. Matisse followed the same method. "I express space and the objects in it as naturally as if I had only sea and sky before me, i. e. the most natural things in the world. This explains why I have not the least trouble in achieving unity ; I let it come quite naturally."

the protest launched in the Cathedral of Wittenberg had not lost its appeal in lands where the Counter-Reformation had been resisted. It was not, however, in the countries in which Protestantism first had taken root that painting voiced that protest ; there were no successors to the German Masters of the sixteenth century. The best artistic interpretation of Protestantism was to be found in Holland. As against the triumphant despotisms of Paris and Madrid, the Batavian Republic maintained a sort of civic liberalism whose limitations were more or less exactly reflected in its art, which severely ruled out the traditional themes of painting. Religious—or rather clerical—influence was outlawed. The Reformation had turned the churches into temples and stripped them bare. Though the naves painted by Saenredam still retained some hints of the invisible Presence in their lofty solitudes, they were a far cry from the churches at Antwerp where Rubens was painting his vast murals. Artists were not encouraged by official commissions from the Synods to choose their subjects from the Old or New Testaments, and while Rembrandt sometimes employed his talent on religious themes, he did so for his own pleasure and because this gave the greatest scope to a passion for painting

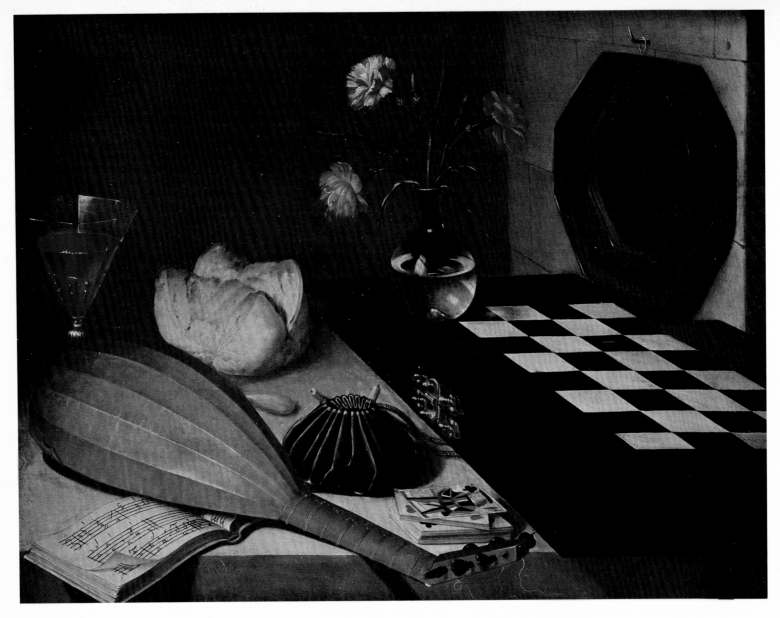

BAUGIN. STILL LIFE WITH CHESSBOARD. (21½ × 28½") LOUVRE, PARIS.

The geometrical lay-out of this composition in diagonals attracts us by its unaffected, slightly naive simplicity ; but its charm, reminiscent of the Primitives, derives rather from the completely free distribution of the objects in the canvas, which are not so much arranged as put there at the painter's whim. In spite of its serious treatment, this subject—a 'Vanitas' — is really only an amusing riddle in which the artist hints at rather than indicates the five senses. This turn of mind, allusive and symbolical in the tradition of the Middle Ages, is close to that of the Surrealists with their wordplays and punning.

which could only be content with subjects of the highest order. Otherwise, biblical painting in Holland broke completely with the exhilaration of the Baroque painters and their riot of color and movement. In it, there was always a touch of the underlying sorrow, that sense of oppression under a load of misfortune, which Protestantism had brought to the surface. Its lighting always came from the interior, which never seemed remote or deep enough to reflect the infinite. Mythological inspiration was frowned upon even more severely. It seemed as though the Renaissance, when it revived the happy forms of a pagan paradise and a vague pantheism taken over from ancient Hellas, and brought back to the world its joy in the naked loveliness of the human body, had done its work in vain. While in Flemish art the female nude was an irresistible challenge to the male to conquer and seduce, that is to fulfil his natural desires, Dutch

HENDRICK VAN STREECK (1659-1713). STILL LIFE. LOUVRE, PARIS.

The miracle of cunning in this still life lies in the fact that, despite a remarkably disciplined construction, in which the colors counterbalance the forms, it is really in an unstable equilibrium, instinct with life. The verticals of the candlestick and the glass seem to be holding back the objects swept forward by the fall of the table-cover. Corresponding to this difficult feat of balance is the perfect harmony of the colors, the cold tones of the silverware balancing the warmth of the material.

art always divided man against himself. The appalling loneliness of the 'Regentessen' of the Haarlem Almshouse, can be sensed even in their bony, clutching hands. And the simmering rage, the agony of suspense weighing on the *Conspiracy of Claudius Civilis* and ravaging the faces of the conspirators, show the distress of man abandoned to his fate even more eloquently than the most harrowing Baroque crucifixions. A society far more concerned with the safety of its merchant fleets than with making war except in grave necessity, would not have seen much point in paintings extolling the triumphs of monarchy in the heroic manner. Men were what really mattered—men who made their money and were satisfied with the comfortable feeling that they had done their duty—and, after them, the object, the simple, homely object, reflection of man and mysterious gleam of God, to whom it owed its being. The object opened up a world in which painting could move freely, no longer acting as a vehicle of political glorification, religious ecstasy or sensual appeal, but solely as itself. This discovery of the everyday things around him held no less pleasure for man than Rubens' crowded, carnally voluptuous world. From this discovery, Dutch painting went on to isolate certain favored forms or things, which gradually rose from the status of accessories to that of the sole subject of the picture. This taste for the ordinary domestic object was one of the traditional features of Flemish painting. Van Eyck was the first to give the accessory this function of reality and primacy. *Genre* painting found its most perfect expression in the still lifes of the century. It must be admitted that such themes became so widespread as to lose variety through over-repetition, and the painters' scrupulous objectivity of execution made them, to all intents and purposes, anonymous.

As against the opulence of Flanders, where a still life chiefly meant the promise or memories of a banquet, the Dutch gained a more purely pictorial effect through their sober, less provocative treatment of the object *per se*. This was the beginning of a taste for 'abstraction' which was to develop and reach its climax in Vermeer. It well may be that the Dutch painters were influenced by considerations similar to those which later led Cézanne and Braque to their tectonic compositions in which the contact of man with the universe is symbolized in contacts of forms and colors alone. Not only had the object, treated simply as a pretext for painting, nothing specially rare or attractive about it, but it was whittled down to something even less conspicuous by artists who stressed only its minor qualities. Flowers, fruits, glasses and overturned goblets lost all vitality and became merely 'things.' The effect of this geometrical reduction was to emphasize effects of spatial balance or unbalance and the interplay of forms between each other; the relationship of lines generally arranged in an intentionally stimulating way, extremely simplified in the background of the picture, but livelier, more varied in the foreground; the relations between carefully contrasted colors giving an impression of airiness because strongly telling out against dark backgrounds; broadly planned composition combined with a subtler organization of details, which often produces an appearance of disorder, accentuated by the use of rather harsh colors. In the work of W. Claes Heda and Davidsz de Heem, as in that of Van Streeck and Pieter Claes, a set purpose to escape from the anecdotal is plain to see. Although the various schools preserved the tradition of the provincial craftsman to such an extent that it is difficult to distinguish between their painters, it would be a mistake to exaggerate their homogeneity ; Amsterdam, dominated by Rembrandt, with its Maes and Fabritius, was unlike Utrecht where Davidsz de Heem held sway, and differed again from Claes's Haarlem. Yet with them all, the refusal to subordinate painting to narrative, to indulge in casual description, seems to have been something fundamental. Sometimes, indeed, the object serving as the starting-off point for the picture was given a heightened significance. Nor should it be forgotten that in these Protestant lands, ever conscious that their souls were imperiled and hungering for spiritual justification, the exchange of ideas was now proceeding on a European scale. The country of Erasmus was long to be the adopted home of Descartes ; metaphysical symbols were beginning to be expressed in the language of pure objects.

In contrast to these Dutch works, the charm and sweetness of the French still life and the austerity of the Spanish have a more immediate appeal, for the cultured intelligence or for the religious instinct.

The poetic realism of the Le Nains set the key for all the *petits maîtres* who have so deservedly emerged from obscurity during the last half-century. These Sunday painters, who were simply good craftsmen specializing in the still life, suggested rather than described the humble objects they delighted in. There is nothing literary in the art of Louise Moillon or Linard, any more than in the imaginings of Séraphine and Vivin. This meticulous sincerity is so lavish of itself that the painter's very soul is communicated to the objects ; they are no longer merely flowers or fruit but spiritual symbols—objects like Blake's "grain of sand," rife in intimations. Here illusionist realism, of its nature a rejection of reality, is not, as with the Dutch, a means to perfect resemblance, but the projection of a poetic vision of nature on to the canvas. The flowers and fruits are not the natural objects that captivate the eye or tickle the appetite, as with the Flemish painters, but symbols at once of divine beneficence and a life of simple, everyday piety. With the French the still life is imbued with a sort of inner jubilation, while the Spanish express in it a meditative contemplation of God's works and the homage of devout, profoundly serious souls. The mystic life takes its stand on reality, and to the mystic the supernatural is the most living reality of all. Zurbaran's objects, painted with the utmost objectivity, have a life of their own. The painter gave no thought to devising a sophisticated lay-out for their presentation. They are set out side by side with an archaic, almost brutal frankness. There is no attempt to beguile the senses. Yet the purity of these compositions endows each object with a nobility which, transcending its material aspects, becomes a symbol of eternity.

This notion of the object as conveying sensual or spiritual overtones was a typically XVIIth-century creation, but it has acquired contemporary significance thanks to Cézanne, Cubism and Surrealism. Could not André Breton's definition of the "poem-object" apply to many of these still lifes : "A composition that sets out to combine the resources of poetry and plastic art and gambles on their power of reciprocal exaltation ?"

VERMEER

Even more than the still life, the interior was dear to the hearts of Dutch painters, for it expressed the tranquil existence of a people remaining, as much by tradition as by necessity, faithful to the domestic scene. But it was left to the two masters of Delft, Jan Vermeer and Pieter de Hooch, to give it its definitive expression. Despite his present worldwide fame, Jan Vermeer was almost unrecognized for two centuries. The credit for rescuing him from comparative oblivion is due to a Frenchman, Théophile Thoré-Bürger (1866). As regards his life, we know only the principal

VERMEER (1632-1675). WOMAN ASLEEP, CA. 1656. DETAIL.
METROPOLITAN MUSEUM OF ART, NEW YORK.

Vermeer's construction consists of straight lines and flat surfaces. These components overlap and interlock, forming parallel lines or angles. Perspective is broken up by the systematic distortion of objects in space, chiefly in order not to hollow the flat surface of the canvas.

VERMEER (1632-1675). YOUNG WOMAN AT A CASEMENT, CA. 1658-1660. (17×15″) METROPOLITAN MUSEUM
OF ART, NEW YORK.

Vermeer's light is like no other. He was familiar with Rembrandt's chiaroscuro, but it was the light of day he wished
to paint. Here this light is diffused through the window held ajar, reflected on the wall at the back and refracted on the
headdress, building it up in wide planes and emphasizing the spirituality of the face, which contrasts with the robust body
imprisoned in its heavy dress.

VERMEER (1632-1675). GIRL IN A RED HAT, CA. 1664. (10×7″) NATIONAL GALLERY, WASHINGTON.

Here, for once, Vermeer enters Rembrandt's domain. The lurid glow of the red hat strikes a contrast with the cold range of colors in the *Young Woman with a Flute*. The tapestry in the background absorbs the light instead of diffusing it and projects the strange headdress, plunging the subject's features into shadow, forward into full light. The density of the air is unusual in Vermeer and the light no longer binds the face in a magic sheen, but yields it up to us.

dates : birth at Delft in 1632, death in 1675, and the records of his creditors. In the absence of documentation, we have to turn to his early works to trace his kinship with the Utrecht followers of Caravaggio and particularly Ter Brugghen. The last pictures of his senior, Carel Fabritius, who died in Delft in 1654, no doubt influenced his methods and gave them a new direction.

Alone, or almost alone, among his contemporaries, he freed himself from the *genre* subject and the narrative painting practiced by Jan Steen, Ter Borch and Van Ostade—no alehouse brawls or grinning apes for him. His favorite subject is a woman reading a letter or standing at a window. If she should turn round when you come in, her faraway, incurious eyes will scarcely see you. This subtle sense of intimacy springs from a real joy in home life, and the atmosphere is one of peacefulness, contented domesticity, and calm, unruffled days. Yet somehow in Vermeer's pictures we always feel a vague unease, a faint undertone of suspense, as though some event at once hoped-for and uncertain were impending. The map on the wall tells of journeys, the geographer bends in a dream over his globe, the wife reads the letter from her absent husband and the woman glimpses her returning lover. These calm Dutch homes shelter a trance-bound life of perfect peace, smooth faces, quiet eyes reflecting a mirage of happiness, distant landscapes poised between earth and sky, daydreams of escape, yet the assurance of a tranquil present.

Against their unchanging background, the figures take on allegorical significance. There is always the same confined room with light-hued walls, the same window-panes shedding a cold light, like the reflection of snow, on familiar objects—the colorful mosaic of a Turkish carpet, the lion's heads on the furniture—and the same girl or young woman, on whom the painter has gazed so often and so long that she has become an idealized, almost abstract figure. In any case, the actual subject meant less to Vermeer than his wonderful technique, which enabled him to model in light without imparting any heaviness to the shadows. Perhaps he had learnt something from Carel Fabritius' fine brushwork, but this does not explain that extraordinary color saturation which is his unique discovery, the hall-mark of his genius. We see this when we scrutinize his works : he used pure colors almost exclusively, cool tones, with a predilection for yellow and blue. If he needs a touch of red in his composition, he tones down its brilliance with brown or orange, so as to avoid striking a 'warm' note. To give modeling and to bring his surfaces to life, he uses small decisive strokes ; sometimes their vibrant color animates the tone, sometimes they bring out the structure of a hand or the granulation of a loaf placed on the table. Whether the impasto is prominent, as in the Amsterdam *Milkmaid* or scarcely visible owing to the smoothness of the surface, the treatment is always the same. Shadows are always colored and translucent ; the Amsterdam *Woman Reading* is a monochrome in blue with the merest hint of brown and just two touches of yellow. The *Head of a Young Girl* at the Hague Museum is modeled entirely in green as regards the shadows, and tells out against a background of the same hue ; this is undoubtedly

what brings out so effectively the blue of the turban and the yellow of the dress. More than any other painter, Vermeer loved pure colors, which he juxtaposed with great virtuosity and such delicacy that the startling nature of the procedure is not immediately perceived. It may be wondered whether the blue of the trees in the *View of Delft*—a strange enough color when you come to think of it—is, as some suppose, due to the effect of time or is rather a piece of deliberate 'Impressionism.'

In complete contrast to Rembrandt's strongly dramatic lighting,

VERMEER (1632-1675). YOUNG WOMAN WITH A FLUTE, CA. 1664. (8×7″) NATIONAL GALLERY, WASHINGTON.

Light, mingling with color, gives form to persons and things. Here, the light comes from the side of the picture, lighting up half the face, redoubling its intensity on the white surfaces, such as the collar and the ermine on the bodice and cuffs, and flooding the flesh with softer tones. On the dark garment, it is indicated by deep blues. The left-hand side is scarcely touched by light or its reflected gleams.

Vermeer's is so precise and true that it succeeds, thanks to the artist's consummate skill, in giving the exact impression of daylight. Vermeer's atmosphere is indefinable in terms of purely visual experience ; only poetic or musical equivalence can give a notion of it. The objects at once absorb and diffuse it ; molded in the impalpable vibration of the light, the figures seem mysteriously to incarnate it.

A picture is not merely an impression, but should be an organized construction. Vermeer's lay-out conforms to the proportions of the 'Golden Section,' but it is also directed by an inner vision, less apparent but reaching further than any purely geometrical arrangement. After an early venture (in the *Sleeping Servant*) into the realm of deep perspective so dear to Pieter de Hooch, the painter finally decided to restrict himself to narrowly confined interiors. The whitewashed wall at the back leaves no possibility of escape ; it is always squarely facing the spectator and parallel to the planes of the picture. The other walls of the room—or idealized box—are only visible in part. Usually there is only the lefthand wall, and very rarely the ceiling. The floor, a checkerboard of stone or marble, provides the third axis of this illusory space by means of its diagonals, or, when this device becomes useless, the furniture alone is used to indicate the recession of the planes up to the shadow of the most distant article of furniture on the wall at the back. The intersection of the dominant verticals and horizontals is echoed in a subtle interplay of rectangles : pictures on the wall, chair-backs, windowframes or the lines of a harpsichord, while the mass of the table serves as a clue to the dimensions of the room and gives this enclosed world its exact proportions.

Pieter de Hooch, who lived in Delft from 1654 to 1662, was Vermeer's neighbor, but nevertheless preserved an independent outlook. The paths of these two painters ran parallel, and the former seems to have borrowed from the latter only when his own inspiration dried up. The space he explores has greater depth, all doors open and outside is the courtyard with its little garden overlooked by the high tower of the Oude Kerke. Such is the setting for his characters—servants going about their household tasks in the morning, or gentlemen and ladies gathered in the best room in the afternoon. There is nothing here of Vermeer's shut-in world or his soft, modulated lighting. Often coming from in front, the light spreads everywhere, lending warmth to the big paved rooms, and stressing the warm, melodious vibration of a red skirt, yet without in the least disturbing the delightful serenity of the atmosphere.

In addition to the fact that Vermeer today seems to be very close to us in feeling, his remarkable affinities with certain French traditions led the Goncourts to say that his art stood for the French ideal. We should be hard put to it to define this somewhat

"The setting is an abstract ground in which the door (despite the oblique line) links up with the curtain, the chair and the wall, which almost merge into each other. The 'Intimists' would have treated this spatial recession corridor-wise, following the canons of a set perspective, and with regressive values ; Vermeer treats the wall at the back as a backcloth impermeable as a shutter. Between two planes, within a space described by some as 'cubist,' he paints the servant, to whom the broad sweep of the style and the intensity of the tones give the solidity of a caryatid, and the woman playing the guitar, whose paradoxically massive lightness and almost bovine gaze make us forget that her face is built up like those of the *Young Woman at a Casement* and the *Woman weighing Pearls*. The tiles extending from the door to the two women, and harmonizing so well with the sandals and domestic objects which create a well-defined depth, seem the very symbol of the work. The letter has no importance, and the women none. Nor has the concrete world in which the letter is being delivered ; for that world has been transmuted into painting." (André Malraux)

VERMEER (1632-1675). THE LOVE LETTER, CA. 1666. (17¼ × 15¼″)
RIJKSMUSEUM, AMSTERDAM.

VERMEER (1632-1675). VIEW OF DELFT, CA. 1658. (35½ × 46″) MAURITSHUIS, THE HAGUE.

"Everything should be placed in perspective so that each side of every object or plane is directed towards a central point. Lines parallel to the horizon give breadth, i. e. a cross-section of nature. Lines perpendicular to the horizon give depth. Now nature is more depth than surface, hence the necessity of introducing a sufficient number of blue touches among the reds and yellows, which represent the vibrations of light, in order to let in the air." (Cézanne)

unstable ideal, whose ingredients seem so often contradictory—an ideal both of order and of freedom, at once intuitive and guided by Reason. Certainly, Vermeer's sensitive appreciation of women and his subtle deference to them belong to the pure French tradition of courtly love. The striking similarities between his genius and that of Chardin

RUISDAEL (1620-1682). VIEW OF HAARLEM. (20½ × 25½″) BERLIN MUSEUM.

The masses of billowing cloud have their complements on the ground in patches of light and shade. "No one ever led the eye from foreground to background with greater competence We can step into this world and move about in it. We can see right to the back of it ; and one is almost tempted to raise one's head to take the measure of the sky." (Fromentin).

or Corot endear him all the more to us, while his happy gift for bodying forth the invisible kingdom of the mind approximates him to Proust and Bergson. The sense of permanence which we find in Vermeer is associated with the luminous quality implicit in his color, and his rediscovery helped to confirm the Impressionists and even the Cubists in their desire to suggest eternity in the moment.

DUTCH LANDSCAPE

The 'object' is the result of long hours of human industry, and on nature man expends long days of patient toil. Just as the trance-bound scenes of Vermeer are a development of the still life, the landscape is simply the transposition of the Dutch interior to the world outside. The map hanging on the wall, like the pattern in the carpet, is an abstract indoors landscape, but through the open window nature invites to solitary walks or truant escapades.

At the beginning of the XVIIth century, Dutch landscape was still only feeling its way, and it soon became bogged in the puerilities of men like Momper and Coninxloo. Hercules Seghers freed it and gave it its proper direction, treating it as a portrait rather than a landscape, as a reflection of the Dutch genius rather than the obvious aspect of some agreeable scene of nature. Seghers' vision, which, as displayed in his engravings, had a hallucinatory quality rather like that of Max Ernst and a severity no less naïve than that of Bauchant, was to inspire Rembrandt. His romantic feeling was not merely a literary fiction as with his predecessors, who had used the Ardennes or the Alps as pretexts for extravagant yet completely formal compositions. Seghers, on the other hand, revealed what they seemed so anxious to hide, namely the inner life of nature. The landscape was transformed : from being vertical, it became horizontal, and from being wild and rugged, it became smooth and calm. No longer do we find those artfully composed masses of rocks poised in precarious balance ; we see the long, wide, sleeping plain with its far horizons, land and water merging into the vastness of the sky. Here

HERCULES SEGHERS (1589-BEFORE 1628). RHENEN AND CANERA TOWER. (10½ × 14″) BERLIN MUSEUM.

This portrayal of infinitude, instead of the over-crowded backgrounds of the XVIth century, was the Dutch solution of the problems which Poussin and Claude were setting themselves in France. The latter were more concerned with light, whereas here the artist aims at rendering space. Segher's vision is undoubtedly the most realistic and scientific of all. Arranged in orderly fashion, it proceeds by a series of successive planes, and succeeds optically in achieving something like what a photograph would show us.

The composition is of a rather surprising kind : a road facing us and cutting the canvas clumsily enough in the middle, thin tufted trees bordering it symmetrically, ditches running parallel to it, a path cutting it at right-angles, a nursery of rosebushes and shrubs planted in straight lines. This landscape of an almost geometrical severity is certainly not picturesque in the traditional sense. But the brown of the vegetation and the yellowish grey of the road form a delicate harmony with the subdued blue of the faintly clouded sky. The way in which the water reflects the sky in a duller range of color is amazingly accurate as to its values and tones. And the execution, of an astonishing breadth and firmness, is in perfect keeping with the subject. Forgetting his usual watermills for once, here Hobbema anticipates the Impressionists in his interpretation of space, and he has imparted to the lopped trees, trimmed and mutilated as they are, a sedate grandeur.

the dynamic quality of the landscape is less superficially apparent ; it lies deeper and is felt more strongly. Behind it we can sense the creative, constantly evolving spirit of the Northern genius. Rembrandt admired Seghers and owned eleven of his pictures. Indeed, owing to Rembrandt's greater fame, works of his less well-known equals were attributed to him. The infinite sought after by Seghers in landscape and by Rembrandt in the portrait was realized by Vermeer in his scenes of Delft. The silence of the little streets matched the painter's own serenity ; the familiar landscape gladdened him like the sight of a beloved face. All eternity is here : in the sky's reflection on the canal, in the smooth map spread under the geographer's compass. But as painting is a living thing, it cannot be maintained at such a pitch of perfection and the balance Vermeer thus imparted to it was unstable. A moment is held in suspense, then the present must resume its ineluctable course. Man might have disappeared from the landscape but he was more sensitive to it than ever. He could be proud of his conquests, not the least of which was nature. And his vision of it was at once an assertion of his supremacy and of his independence.

It was no mere coincidence that the land of Rembrandt, Vermeer and Ruisdael was the first to discover the laws of optics and make human sight the *sine qua non* of understanding. A Dutch optician, Lippersheim, invented the telescope at the beginning of the century and another Dutchman, Jansen, invented the microscope. These discoveries, which carried the vanishing point to infinity and also enlarged the foreground practically to infinity, caused an upheaval in the world that Pascal was to survey and define. While these two inventions did not actually add a new dimension to space, they enlarged the visual field. And not only the vision was enlarged, but the spirit, too. For St Thomas, seeing was believing ; henceforth seeing was knowing, confirmation of the authority of the scientist who knew and of the painter who saw. Man in relation to nature became free and independent, since he imposed his own vision on it. When Louis XIV had his palace decorated with the famous mirrors, he was not merely yielding to a narcissistic desire to multiply the sight of his reflected self ; he felt a need to assert his authority and ensure its visual confirmation. The mirrors in the Dutch interiors and the quiet canals reflecting the sky in Van Goyen's landscapes were, in their smaller way, an equivalent of the Hall of Mirrors at Versailles. Thus Holland saw itself reflected in its own setting of sky and water.

Van Goyen's landscapes are vast, colorless, and as neutral as abstractions. This way of seeing the world, reduced to bare essentials, is typically Dutch. The anecdotal is ruled out—indeed it would be pointless. To dwell on details, to tell the whole story, would be out of place in a world three-quarters cloud and spanned by a great river. This compromise between eternity and the moment anticipates the discoveries of Impressionism.

With Ruisdael, the landscape is just a *motif* of the ordinary kind ; but in the hands of this austere, original painter, it becomes a carefully considered, pregnant *motif*. "The landscape dies away upon the void, the water on the open plain lures down the sky to meet it." Yet in this elemental solitude, the human element, the soul, makes its presence felt ; here and there the triangle of a steeple or a sail strikes a shrill, vibrant note. And above the rolling plain a huge cumulus-cloud, keystone of the celestial vault, looms heavily. This scene of grandeur and aloofness, rendered with a low-pitched palette confined to browns, beiges and autumn hues, is imbued with a haunting sadness, a vague emotion foreshadowing the hopeless yearnings of Obermann and René. Modern man was already trying to discover correspondences between nature and his personal feelings, and soon he was to foist them on it. This new humanizing of the elements—air, water and the fertile earth—was his last triumph ; but it laid the sentimental traps into which romantics were to fall, the "pathetic fallacy."

Hobbema harked back to a more accurate realism, but for this he had to sacrifice the mysterious poetry of landscape. That elemental hush in which a 'still, small voice' made itself heard was ended by the scrutiny of the analyst and illustrator. Nature is no longer a *motif* but an objective, and—as in a badly-focussed photograph—the composition falls to pieces, the sky is flattened out. A single work lends luster to Hobbema : *The Avenue*, where, under a low sky ribboned by ragged poplars, a road winds into the heart of Holland. It was an invitation, and taken as such by Gainsborough and Constable, and, after them, by Pissarro and Sisley. Quite obviously it pointed the way to Sisley's *Sloping Path* in the Caillebotte Collection. Yet this call, heard only by XIXth-century English landscape painters and the French Impressionists, left contemporaries unmoved. Once a subject becomes a stock theme, its original intention is falsified, it loses all individuality. By the end of the century the spiritual unity given it by Seghers and Vermeer had vanished from Dutch painting. There were painters of seascapes, of architecture, of urban and country scenes. They were story-tellers and illustrators, agreeable enough, but without any real originality. When it so happened that one of them showed a spark of individuality, he soon extinguished it by repeating whatever pleased his public. And there were many such. Two of them deserve to be mentioned because they are genuinely sincere, and have a lesson for our times. Saenredam specialized in painting church architecture. Though he was less erudite and more naïve than Emmanuel de Witte, his interiors of churches, stripped of the divine presence, yet seeming to await its improbable return, have retained in their high, white walls a lingering warmth which the minister in his pulpit seems to be trying to keep up. In the same way Post's landscapes have a quaint interest, because they show us a Westerner's response to the discovery of the exotic.

> *Tu te souviens, Rousseau, du paysage aztèque,*
> *Des forêts où poussaient la mangue et l'ananas,*
> *Des singes répandant tout le sang des pastèques,*
> *Et du blond empereur qu'on fusilla là-bas.*

It would be pleasant to imagine that Post's Brazil was as fanciful as the Douanier's Mexico as pictured by Apollinaire ; but he was too naïve, too conscientious to tamper with what he thought to be the facts—and indeed it is this sincerity in his work that moves us.

The many successors of the late XVIIth-century Dutch painters, with their well-defined limits and subjects, almost endangered the whole future of painting. Which goes to show that, when the subject, however slight (and in this case it was very slight indeed), becomes more important than the painting (and here it was simply a clever knack), art discards its ideals, and in a sense commits suicide. The prestige of French painting—no more than an illusion, since it was guided and controlled so strongly—hastened the end of the Golden Century. It is significant that more than a century was to pass before the great tradition and the true spirit of XVIIth-century Dutch painting enjoyed a second blooming in an atmosphere of freedom—this time in France, with Boudin, Monet, Sisley.

THE LEGACY OF THE CENTURY

Works of art of earlier periods constitute a background which always influences the outlook of contemporary art-lovers, while, for the artist, they furnish a repertory of signs that always modify and may even transform his own creations. By way of conclusion, it may be well to say something of the fluctuations of the taste for XVIIth-century painting in subsequent centuries, to show its influence on later generations and to illustrate, with a few concrete examples, this vicarious immortality of forms.

At the end of the XVIIth century, Rubens' art emerged triumphant from its struggle with the upholders of Poussin's classicism and the Academy. Louis XIV patronized Rubens' followers, Coypel and Jouvenet, and purchased the *Kermesse* (1685), which was later copied by Watteau (1709), while the dilettanti now lost interest in Poussin. Painting developed liveliness and gaiety, and instinctively steered clear of masters whose ideas were adjudged too austere by contemporary standards. Boucher and Fragonard were inspired by Albani's charming themes and cupids ; Murillo's rather mawkish piety pleased everyone. At the same time, a half-reluctant taste for naturalism tended to popularize Dutch painting and its homely subjects, less on their artistic merits than for their familiar appeal. Engravings of Van Ostade's works by Bernard Picard (1730) influenced Chardin. The success of the insipidities of Gerard Dou and Jan Steen corresponded to Diderot's bourgeois aesthetic, and matched that of Greuze's moralistic *bambocciate*. A new idea, or perhaps we should say a tendency, now entered French art, which began, surprisingly enough under the circumstances, to feel a need to have significance and a message. The vogue of Ruisdael, Van Goyen and Van de Velde, whose works were included in the royal collections, can be explained by Rousseau and the fashionable cult of romantic nature. At the same time, the return to Antiquity —for poverty had acquired snob-value and simplicity was *à la mode*—favored the plainness of Le Sueur's art. Quite possibly Poussin would have come back into fashion, if the outbreak of the Revolution had not given art a wholly new direction.

And now the Italian masterpieces found their way to the Louvre, along with fifty-four paintings by Rubens, thirty-three by Rembrandt, and Potter's famous *Bull*, while the Soult and Favier Spanish collections were built up. Young painters began to haunt the Louvre to learn the lessons of the masters, and Gros and, later, Delacroix were thus to be inspired by Rubens. But middle-class taste was little if at all affected by the political upheaval ; it kept to its old ideas and was naturally drawn to the Dutch 'Little Masters,' who amply satisfied its taste for entertainment and the picturesque. It was not until Louis-Philippe's reign that a sudden interest in Spanish painting sprang up. In 1837, Taylor brought no less than four hundred and twelve canvases from Spain, and the King lent them to the Louvre, where they were exhibited. It was then that Zurbaran's work came into prominence. The Aguado and Soult sales (1843 and 1852 respectively) and the sale of Louis-Philippe's private collection in London (1853) once more drew attention to the Spanish masters and confirmed the vogue for Murillo, inevitably linked with sentimental piety. This was the time when Manet developed an enthusiasm for Velazquez, copied one of his pictures, and went to the Prado in quest of confirmation for his Impressionism. The Louvre acquired several of Ribera's paintings, and his realism inspired the group which called itself the 'School of Madrid' and consisted of Bonnat, Henri Regnault, Carolus-Duran and T.-A. Ribot.

The independent, democratic nature of Dutch painting fitted in with the mood prevailing in France (an aftermath of the social idealism of 1848) during the last half of the century. No doubt, the reasons for the return to favor of these *genre* paintings were not purely artistic; however, Thoré-Bürger's *Histoire de l'Art Hollandais* (1861), Fromentin's *Maîtres d'Autrefois* (1876) and Marcel Proust's *Portraits de Peintres* (1896) revealed their true originality. For similar literary or political reasons, there was a movement in favor of the French painters of reality. At approximately the same time, Thoré-Bürger and Champfleury discovered Vermeer (1866) and the Le Nains (1862). And this return to the living art of the XVIIth century was sponsored by the addition to the Louvre collection of *Peasants at their Meal* (1869), *The Cart* (1879) and *The Family Reunion* (1887).

By repercussion, Poussin also benefited by these changed conditions. While the Institute was pleased, the 'Salon' painters were no doubt astonished that, following Cézanne, who wished "to do Poussin again, after nature," the Cubists sought endorsement of their theories from the master of Classicism. Also the growing taste for the 'Sunday painters' was perhaps not unconnected with the new appreciation of the XVIIth-century masters of reality. An extensive literature on the subject developed, including the scholarly studies of Paul Jamot, Charles Sterling and Georges Isarlo, F. G. Pariset's monograph on Georges de La Tour (abruptly rescued from obscurity), while the publications of the Poussin Society rectified the current conceptions of the XVIIth century, hitherto overshadowed by the glory of Louis XIV, and proved that, as well as being a century of great material splendor, it was also, and pre-eminently, one of great creations in art.

BIOGRAPHICAL AND BIBLIOGRAPHICAL NOTICES

ALBANI, FRANCESCO.

Bologna 1578-1660, Italian School.

Albani was a pupil of Carracci and, after 1616, devoted himself entirely to landscapes, in which he showed a feeling for nature rather rare in his period. His painting usually had some mythological content, but it consisted mainly of Cupids flying through the air or playing with nymphs and was thus a pleasant variation of the traditional themes. His smiling landscapes, finely painted foliage and bright skies appealed to XVIIIth-century art-lovers and painters. He was greatly admired by Boucher and Fragonard and something of his Anacreontic gusto is to be found in Prud'hon's paintings.

ARPINO, GIUSEPPE CESARI, known as IL CAVALIERE D'.

Arpino 1560-1640, Italian School.

A prolific decorator and the protégé of Popes Gregory XIII and Clement VIII. His ease of execution and the brilliance of his canvases did not always make up for the weaknesses of his drawing, but his reputation equaled that of the Carracci. He painted the ceiling of the Contarelli Chapel at San Luigi dei Francesi in Rome, where Caravaggio painted scenes from the life of St Matthew.

Bibl.: RINALDIS, A. de. *D'Arpino e Caravaggio* in *Bollettino d'arte*. 1935-1936, pp. 577-580.

BASCHENIS, EVARISTO.

Bergamo 1617-1677, Italian School.

Son of a painter, Baschenis, who entered the priesthood, specialized in painting still lifes. He was much admired for his delightful paintings of musical instruments in discreetly contrasted tones, and also for the originality of his composition. Like his friend Jacques Courtois, he also painted battle-scenes with life-size figures.

BAUGIN.

French School.

This realistic painter, about whom nothing is known, not even his Christian name, has been confused with his namesake Lubin Baugin, an imitator of the Bolognese painters and of Guido Reni. Two still lifes, one in the Louvre and one in the Spada Gallery, Rome, place him among the painters of Vouet's and Vignon's generation, who made the journey to Rome and were influenced there by Caravaggio's first manner.

Bibl.: ISARLO, G. *La nature morte à l'exposition d'Amsterdam* in *Formes XXXII*. 1933. — Catalogue of the Exhibition *Peintres de la Réalité*. Paris 1934.

BROUWER, ADRIAEN.

Oudenarde 1605 - Antwerp 1638, Flemish School.

Landscape and *genre* painter. Probably a pupil of Frans Hals. Nearly all the themes of his *genre* paintings deal with the life of the country inn: drinking-bouts, brawls, card-parties, etc. His portrayal of scenes of rustic life at first smacked of caricature, but was later toned down: his psychological observation grew keener, while his color became more subtle and his composition gained in ease and strength. The very free treatment of his best pictures is like that of Hals in those of his paintings which anticipate Impressionism.

Bibl.: SCHMIDT-DEGENER, F. *Adriaen Brouwer et son évolution artistique*. Brussels 1908.

BRUEGHEL, JAN, DE VELOURS.

Brussels 1568 - Antwerp 1625, Flemish School.

A painter of *genre* scenes, landscapes, animals, flowers and fruits. Trained in Italy (1593-1596) and in Germany. His brilliant narrative art has affinities with the miniature. In his landscapes, he followed the tradition of Peter Brueghel the Elder. He collaborated with Rubens on a number of occasions and painted landscape backgrounds for Van Balen, Momper, Frans Francken and P. Neefs.

Bibl.: DENUCI, J. *Lettres et documents concernant Jan Brueghel*. Antwerp 1934.

CARAVAGGIO, MICHELANGELO MERISI.

Caravaggio 1573 - Porto Ercole 1610, Italian School.

From the age of eleven, Caravaggio was a pupil of Simone Peterzano in Milan. After four years' apprenticeship, he went to Rome where, for a time, he assisted the painters Gramatica and then Arpino. As a protégé of Cardinal del Monte, who offered him hospitality, he painted the 'bright' works of his first period: *Bacchus*, the *Magdalen Repentant* and the *Girl playing the Lute*. Through his patron, he got in touch with Cardinal Contarelli's executor who commissioned the decoration of a chapel at San Luigi dei Francesi. A first version of *St Matthew and the Angel*, painted in 1590, was refused, but the *Vocation of St Matthew* (ca. 1593) and his *Martyrdom* (ca. 1595), together with the new version of *St Matthew* (ca. 1598), were successful and aroused the interest of such art-lovers as Vincenzo Giustiniani, Ciriaco Mattei, the Barberinis and the Massinos.

About 1600, Caravaggio completed two pictures for the Cerasi Chapel at Santa Maria del Popolo: *The Conversion of St Paul* and the *Crucifixion of St Peter*. Between 1603 and 1605, he completed the *Madonna of the Pilgrims* and the *Entombment* now in the Vatican Gallery. Then, owing to his reckless, extravagant way of life, and the brawls in which he was involved, he was obliged to leave Rome for a time.

In 1606, the *Death of the Virgin* was refused by the Brothers of Santa Maria della Scala. The picture was later to be acquired by the Duke of Mantua, while Cardinal Scipione Borghese, not content with acquiring the *Madonna of the Ostlers*, obtained a *St John the Baptist*, a *St Jerome* and a *David* from the painter. In the same year (1606) occurred the murder of Ranuccio Tomassoni, which obliged Caravaggio, himself seriously wounded, to flee from Rome and hide in Prince Colonna's estate, before seeking refuge at Naples, where he painted seven 'Works of Mercy.' While his production did not slow down, his works were often freer and more hasty in treatment following his stay in Malta, where he painted two portraits of the Grand Master Adolf de Wignacourt. After another fight, he had to flee once more, this time to Syracuse, where he left an *Entombment of Santa Lucia* (1608). He next went to Messina, where he painted the *Resurrection of Lazarus* and the *Adoration of the Shepherds*, and then to Palermo, where he painted the *Nativity with St Laurence and St Francis*. Pursued to Naples by his enemies, he still hoped to return to Rome where Cardinal Gonzaga was prepared to obtain a pardon for him, but, on landing at Porto Ercole, he was put in prison and died there of a fever.

Bibl.: FRANCASTEL, P. *Le réalisme de Caravage* in *Gazette des Beaux-Arts*. July-August 1932, pp. 45-62. — ISARLO, G. *Caravage et le Caravagisme européen*, Catalogues. Aix 1941. SCHUDT, L. *Caravaggio*. Vienna 1942. — LONGHI, R. *Ultimi studi sul Caravaggio e la sua cerchia* in *Proporzioni*, I. 1943, pp. 5-63 and 99-102. — VENTURI, L. *Il 'baro' del Caravaggio ritrovato* in *Commentari*. 1950, No. 1, pp. 41-42. LONGHI, R. *Il Caravaggio e la sua cerchia a Milano* in *Paragone*, No. 15. March 1951. Catalogue of the Exhibition of *Caravaggio and his School*. Milan 1951.

CARRACCI, ANNIBALE.

Bologna 1560 - Rome 1609, Italian School.

Together with his cousin Lodovico Carracci (1555-1619) and his brother Agostino, Annibale Carracci founded an Academy at Bologna in 1582 to teach not only painting, but anatomy and the history and theory of art. The pupils worked from life, but the study of the masters was also strongly recommended : Raphael and Michelangelo for drawing and especially Correggio and the Venetians for color. It was an attempt to get away from Mannerism by means of a rational form of instruction which was promptly christened 'Eclecticism.'

In 1597, Annibale was commissioned by Cardinal Odoardo Farnese to decorate the Gallery of the Palace just built by Giacomo della Porta. He worked on it for ten years, and, at first, was helped by his brother Agostino. After the Farnesina and the Palazzo del Te, this was the last great achievement of Renaissance art. Its success was so great that, for two centuries, it was a model for decorators.

The influence of the Academy was even more widespread. Guido Reni, Albani, Domenichino, Guercino and Lanfranc were all trained there and it set the standard for subsequent academic schools. Lebrun's work may be traced back to it. At the same time, new vistas were being opened up by Caravaggio, who died shortly after Annibale Carracci.

Bibl. : FORATTI, A. *I Carracci nella teoria et bella pratica.* Città di Castello 1913. — BODMER, H. *Lodovico Carracci.* Burg 1939.

CHAMPAIGNE, PHILIPPE DE.

Brussels 1602 - Paris 1674, French School.

At the age of nineteen, Champaigne left Flanders, where he had been trained, went to Paris and worked on the decoration of the Luxembourg. A painter of religious pictures and portraits, he gained a great reputation at the court and in Jansenist circles. Despite his Flemish origin, he rapidly absorbed the French outlook, and to such an extent that he became one of the leading representatives of XVIIth-century French art. He proclaimed and stressed the high seriousness of man's soul and form, and succeeded in fusing realistic observation with classical tendencies. His portraits interpret the inner life, the deepest levels of the psyche, which he suggests with admirable discretion.

Bibl. : SKIN, H. *Philippe de Champaigne et ses relations avec Port-Royal.* Société des Beaux-Arts des départements. 1891. — GAZIER. *Philippe et J.-B. de Champaigne.* Paris 1893. — COURTHION, Pierre. *Les Portraits de Philippe de Champaigne* in *L'Art et les artistes.* 1926, vol. XIV.

CLAESZ, PIETER.

Bürgsteinfürt 1597 - Haarlem 1661, Dutch School.

Claesz' favorite subjects were still lifes in which metal and earthenware vases were set side by side with table accessories often arranged on crumpled tablecloths. His compositions are sometimes arbitrary. The yellow of a lemon or the red of wine in a glass were almost the only bright touches he allowed himself in a color-scheme dominated by a limpid brown and a greyish green. His son was the landscape-painter Nicholas Berchem.

CORTONA, PIETRO BERRETTINI.

Cortona 1596 - Rome 1669, Italian School.

Architect, painter, church-builder and painter of such famous ceilings as that of the Palazzo Barberini. His great skill in decoration gained him important commissions at the Pitti Palace. His pleasant style and the rounded faces of the women he painted are reminiscent of Domenichino and won him the appreciation of the XVIIIth-century French painters.

Bibl. : MUNOZ, A. *Pietro da Cortona.* Rome 1921.

COURTOIS, JACQUES, known as LE BOURGUIGNON.

St. Hippolyte 1621 - Rome 1676, French School.

The romantic life of this curious man, who lived in Rome from fifteen years of age is reflected in his favorite subjects, dramatic battle-pieces, and in his tense, almost extravagant technique. He was influenced by Bamboccio and Salvator Rosa and was Parrocel's master.

Bibl. : BLONDEAU. *L'œuvre de J. Courtois, dit le Bourguignon des Batailles.* 1914. — SALVAGNINI. *I pittori borgognoni Cortese.* Rome 1937.

CUYP, AELBERT.

Dordrecht 1620-1691, Dutch School.

Son of Jacob Gerritz Cuyp. His first landscapes, painted between 1639 and 1645, have affinities with those of Van Goyen. He developed a more original style towards 1650 ; while his subjects remained traditional, his sunny landscapes owe their Italian atmosphere to Jan Both. His very varied paintings—cattle drinking, cows being milked, views of Dordrecht from the harbor or skating scenes—are given their special quality by his warm light. His groups of men on horseback in landscapes with low horizons enabled him to try his hand at portraiture and are his most individual works.

Bibl.: VETH, G. H. *Aelbert Cuyp* in *oud Holland.* 1884, p. 256.

DOMENICHINO, DOMENICO ZAMPIERI.

Bologna 1581 - Naples 1641, Italian School.

A pupil of Denis Calvaert's and then of the Carracci, he cooperated with Annibale Carracci on the decoration of the Farnese Gallery, where his *Girl with Unicorn* bears witness to his early mastery. From 1605, he lived in Rome, made the San Giorgio frescos with Guido Reni and then the decoration of the Aldobiandini Villa at Frascati, with Apollo as the theme, and the series of paintings at the Grotta Ferrata Convent. *Diana's Hunt* in the Borghese Gallery (1625) shows his taste for the type of landscape dear to Poussin, and also a freshness of feeling rare in this period. At Sant' Andrea della Valle, his evangelists on the pendentives of the cupola throw the rest of the decoration (the work of Lanfranc) into the shade. In 1631, he was commissioned to complete the frescos of the Treasury at Naples Cathedral, which Guido Reni had left unfinished. He died there, it is said, from poisoning. Of all the Bolognese painters he was the most sensitive, the most interested in rendering movement and lifelike expression.

Bibl. : SERRA, L. *D. Zampieri.* Rome 1909.

DOU, GERARD.

Leyden 1613-1675, Dutch School.

Portrait and *genre* painter and a pupil of Rembrandt's, whose influence is apparent in the chiaroscuro of his portraits and his early compositions in which the lighting usually comes from a candle or a lamp. His extreme attention to detail made him such a slow worker that he was obliged to give up painting portraits. His characters, whose gestures often seem abrupt, uncouth, are usually seen through a window, engaged in some homely or everyday task—such as cooking or selling vegetables—or in conversation. The increasing importance he gave the inanimate objects in his paintings led him to the still life towards the end of his career. Among his pupils were Frans van Mieris the Elder and Gabriel Metsu.

Bibl. : MARTIN, W. *Gerard Dou, Klassiker der Kunst.* 1913.

DYCK, ANTHONY VAN.

Antwerp 1599 - Blackfriars 1641, Flemish School.

Van Dyck, who came of a family of prosperous merchants, entered Van Balen's studio in 1610, then went to study under Rubens about 1612. After a short stay at Charles I's court, he returned to Antwerp (1621) and painted the *St Martin* in the church at Saventhem. In the same year, he went to Genoa, where he painted a series of family portraits of the Waels, the Durazzos and the Grimaldis. In 1622, he visited Rome, Florence, Bologna, Venice and Mantua, returning to Rome in 1623 and there painting a portrait of Cardinal Bentivoglio, and several religious works. After a further stay in Genoa, he returned to Antwerp in 1624, passing through Aix. Freeing himself from Rubens' influence, he came under the spell of Titian, from whom he took over his dark, warm tones, heavy shadows which give vibration to the light, and the procedure of sacrificing accessories so as to stress the hands and face in a portrait. In 1630 he returned to London, where he became an intimate friend of Charles I, of whom he painted over thirty portraits, in addition to portraits of members of the English aristocracy. These works still show Van Dyck's qualities as a painter, but suffer from over-hasty execution and the necessity of flattering his subjects. He was the founder of the English School and a forerunner of Gainsborough, Reynolds and Lawrence.

Bibl. : FIERENS-GEVAERT. *Van Dyck.* "Grands Artistes." 1904. — SEEMANN, A. *Van Dyck.* Bergamo 1933. — Catalogue, *Rubens et son temps* Exhibition. Paris 1936. IMBOURG. *Van Dyck.* Monaco 1950.

ELSHEIMER, ADAM.

Frankfort 1574 or 1578 - Rome 1610, German School.

At an early age, Elsheimer went to Rome, where he settled and became known as Adamo Tedesco. He studied there, lived with the Dutch painters Lastman and Pinas, who were Rembrandt's first masters ; he influenced Saraceni and was the teacher of David Teniers. His most successful works were small landscapes with mythological or biblical themes, but treated with a very individual idyllic charm. His nightscapes are "full of lurking perils, nervous fears; his chiaroscuros are fraught with hidden treasures and delicate emotion." Thus Focillon has defined the art of Elsheimer, that "tender, patient, deeply meditative dreamer."

Bibl. : DROST, N. *Adam Elsheimer und sein Kreis.* Potsdam 1935.

FABRITIUS, CAREL.

Haarlem ca. 1620-1624 - Delft 1654, Dutch School.

A pupil of Rembrandt. Only a very small number of works which can be definitely attributed to him are known. Of these, his self-portrait at the Boymans Museum, Rotterdam, and the *Goldfinch* at the Mauritshuis, The Hague, are perhaps the most remarkable. The oiliness of his pigment and his use of luminous effects show the influence of his teacher, whereas the relative brightness of his palette and his growing taste for figures telling out against a bright background are sometimes reminiscent of Vermeer. His brother Barent, who was his pupil and Rembrandt's, took his themes from the Bible, mythology and history, but inferior drawing marred his very real talent for painting.

Bibl. : HOFSTEDE DE GROOT. *Jan Vermeer van Delft und Carel Fabritius.* Amsterdam 1906.

FETI, DOMENICO.

Rome 1589 - Venice 1624, Italian School.

A pupil of Cigoli and influenced by Caravaggio, Feti was summoned in 1614 to the court of the Duke of Mantua, whose excellent collection revealed the works of the great Venitians. Always a realist, but handling color more freely than most realists, he played some part in the development of the Venetian School during the closing years of his life.

Bibl. : OLDENBOURG, R. *Domenico Feti.* Rome 1921.

FINSON, LODEWYK, known as FINSONIUS.

Bruges before 1580 - Amsterdam 1617, Flemish School.

Finson went to Rome and Naples at an early age and was struck by the novelty of Caravaggio's art. Thus, his *Resurrection of Christ*, painted in 1610 for the church of St John in Aix, passed, according to old documents, for a copy of a lost work by the master. After another visit to Naples, he returned to Aix, where he painted pictures for churches. He was one of the first Northern painters to be converted to the new form of art and introduced the style of Caravaggio to Provence. Amongst his pupils was the painter Fauchier.

GENTILESCHI, ORAZIO.

Pisa ca. 1565 - London ca. 1647, Italian School.

Gentileschi came to Rome before 1585 ; he had been trained on Mannerist lines but he was among the first to adopt the bright manner of Caravaggio's early work, and he treated it in such a personal way that formerly he was not regarded as a 'Caravaggesque.' He worked at Genoa from 1621 to 1623 and in France, where he stayed for a period of probably two years, before sailing for England in 1626 to become Painter to Charles I. He had a wide influence on XVIIth-century Dutch painting.

GOYEN, JAN VAN.

Leyden 1596 - The Hague 1665, Dutch School.

Van Goyen had a very thorough training under Esaias Van de Velde and other masters. Beginning with rather harshly rendered landscapes, he moved (in or about 1630) towards a monochrome style of painting, in dull browns, his favorite subjects being dunes and thatched cottages. Stretches of water and high cloudy skies were added after 1636. Light also began to play a leading part and yellow and grey-green tones predominated. However, it was not until after 1645 that he adopted a warm brown peculiarly suited for conveying the very special atmosphere of a sodden countryside.

Bibl. : GROSSE, R. *Die holländische Landschaft Kunst. 1600-1650.* 1925, pp. 64-78.

GUERCINO, GIOVANNI FRANCESCO BARBIERI.

Cento 1591 - Bologna 1666, Italian School.

Already famous when he was working in Lodovico Carracci's studio, Guercino visited Venice, where Palma the Younger revealed to him Veronese, Titian and Tintoretto, though he was even more impressed by Caravaggio's use of contrasts. His masterpiece is that great ceiling at the Villa Ludovici representing Aurora's chariot moving through the air above an architectural background. Never before had chiaroscuro given such an intense impression of life and movement in space. He painted many decorations and altarpieces, which, after Guido Reni's death, made him the leading painter in Bologna.

Bibl. : MARANGONI. *Il Guercino.* Florence 1920.

HALS, FRANS.

Antwerp 1580 - Haarlem 1666.

Little is known about the life of this genial, bohemian, happy-go-lucky, yet on occasion obdurate character, but we do know that he was hardly a model of virtue. He started his career as a painter at thirty-six years of age with *Banquet of the Officers of the St Joris Shooting Guild* (1616), in which he embodied all his gifts, almost too copiously, too lavishly. His range of color became brighter and his composition progressively simpler throughout his career, which culminated in his masterpiece The 'Regents' of *the Haarlem Almshouse* (1664).

His portraits are real 'character' paintings; the subjects were chosen from amongst the picturesque, cheerful people with whom he associated ; e.g. the *Merry Trio* (1616), the *Gipsy Girl* (1630) and *Hille Babbe* (1650). His life was a hard one, but his good humor never deserted him and his philosophy of life is in his laughter.

Bibl. : MOES. *Frans Hals ; sa vie, son œuvre.* Brussels 1909. BODE, W. von. *Frans Hals - sein Leben und seine Werke*, 2 vols. Berlin 1914. — GRATZMA. *Frans Hals.* 1938.

HEDA, WILLEM CLAESZ.

Haarlem 1594-1682, Dutch School.

A painter of still lifes in the manner of Pieter Claesz. His soft, silvery range of color is extremely harmonious. He never had Claesz' vigor; he showed more interest in elaborately devised composition.

HEEM, JAN DAVIDSZ DE.

Utrecht 1606 - Antwerp 1684, Dutch School.

Studied under his father David de Heem and B. van der Alst. He was primarily a painter of flowers and fruits, but he also painted still lifes with certain recurring elements : books, musical instruments, glasses, candles, skulls and the like. Though his work at first had some affinities with that of Pieter Claesz, he was influenced by the Flemish painter Daniel Seghers towards the end of his career. His works, which are generally well-constructed and effective in coloring, place him midway between the Flemish and Dutch Schools.

Bibl. : BODE, W. von. *Die Meister der Holländischen und Vlämischen Malerschulen.* 1917, p. 288.

HERRERA, FRANCISCO.

Seville 1576 - Madrid 1656, Spanish School.

Herrera's fantastic, unsociable and eccentric character gave him a reputation which is reflected in his paintings, but their rough violence is actually more superficial than seriously meant. He was in fact little more than a robust disciple of Roella. He favored dramatic and realistic compositions (*Apotheosis of St Hermenegilde*, Louvre), but his best works are certainly *The Idiot* (Calvet Museum, Avignon) and the *Blind Musician*, in the Czernin Collection, Vienna, which has been attributed to him.

HOBBEMA, MEINDERT.

Amsterdam 1638-1709, Dutch School.

A friend and perhaps a pupil of Jacob van Ruisdael. His stock subjects are the wooded dunes of the Haarlem region, pink-roofed mills among tall trees, ruins and views of towns. While his first works are almost indistinguishable from those of his presumptive master, the landscapes he painted in his maturity show a concern for meticulously rendered detail and a use of contrasts of light and shade which are not to be found to the same extent in Ruisdael. His colors are also brighter, more emphatic than those of Ruisdael, who had a preference for greys. He kept repeating the same themes, making no attempt to vary them, and displayed an obvious predilection for water-mills. He seems to have stopped painting after 1667. His fame commenced in England at the close of the XVIIIth century.

Bibl. : BROUILHET, G. *Hobbema.* 1938.

HONTHORST, GERARD VAN.

Utrecht 1590-1656, Dutch School.

After studying under Abraham Bloemaert, Honthorst went to Italy where he was greatly impressed by Caravaggio's powerful handling of light effects. The artificial light—torches, lamps, candles—which he then started to use in his paintings earned him the nickname "Gherardo della Notte." Like Caravaggio and Rubens, he painted large allegorical, mythological and historical compositions. To the former he also owed his half-length card-players and his violinists arranged around a central light. Following his return to Utrecht in 1622, he enjoyed great success as a Society painter and received commissions not only from his own country, but also from London, Denmark and Berlin. From that time onwards the elegant, rather insipid Society portrait bulked ever larger in his output. It is thought that Rembrandt's chiaroscuro may owe something to him.

Bibl. : SCHNEIDER, A. von. *Caravaggio und die Niederländer.* 1933, pp. 21-31.

HOOCH, PIETER DE.

Rotterdam 1629 - Amsterdam after 1684, Dutch School.

After Vermeer, Hooch was the most important *genre* painter of his School. To his master Nicholas Berchem, he owed the treatment of light and color in his first paintings (landscapes with horsemen). His interiors of stables and guard-rooms and scenes of children at play recall Anthonie Palamedesz, but his coloring is richer. He rendered the effect of space by means of intenser coloring and a warmer, more vivid, golden light which he learnt partly from Carel Fabritius. In his dimly lit interiors we are usually shown persons going quickly about their work ; it is their presence, as well as the openings giving glimpses of the outside air, that imparts a sense of spaciousness to these interiors. The masterpieces of his maturity have a quiet, sunny radiance, an atmosphere of calm well-being. His brushwork is light and fluent without the least niggardliness ; the pigment is thin, often translucent. His last works are not so successful ; shadows tend to be opaque and the flesh has an unpleasant bluish tinge.

Bibl. : WALENTINER. *Pieter de Hooch (Klassiker der Kunst).* Stuttgart. 1929.

JORDAENS, JACOB.

Antwerp 1593-1678, Flemish School.

A cloth-merchant's son, Jordaens was apprenticed to Van Noort in 1607 and later married his daughter. He was admitted to the Antwerp Guild of Painters in 1615. His first work, the *Adoration of the Shepherds* (1618) in the Stockholm Museum is typical of his early manner, at once rustic and Caravaggesque. In 1628, he was commissioned to work with Rubens and Van Dyck on the decoration of the Augustinian church at Antwerp and painted his *Martyrdom of St Apollina*. His technique became strongly sculptural and his color acquired a vibrant quality. Nevertheless, under Rubens' influence, his manner became more fluid, more luminous : *The Young Ones twitter as the Old Folks sing, Twelfth Night, The Education of Jupiter* and the *Triumph of Bacchus* date from this period (1624-1635). After 1645 he harked back to his early treatment of light in terms of chiaroscuro : in his *St Yves* (1645), now at the Brussels Museum, and his *Susanna and the Elders* (1653). Following his conversion to Calvinism (1650), he confined himself almost entirely to biblical subjects. *Jesus among the Doctors* (Mainz Museum), painted in 1663, is his greatest and also his largest work. His last canvases, which were influenced by the Dutch, are increasingly Caravaggesque : *The Last Supper* (Antwerp Museum) and the *Triumph of Bacchus* (Brussels Museum).

Bibl. : FIERENS-GEVAERT. *Jordaens, "Grands Artistes."* 1905. — ROOSES, Max. *Jordaens. Sa vie et ses œuvres.* 1926.

JOUVENET, JEAN-BAPTISTE.

Rouen 1644 - Paris 1717, French School.

Studied under his father Laurent Jouvenet and then under Lebrun, but was instinctively drawn towards Rubens. He had a brilliant career and succeeded in combining academic doctrine with living art.

He painted the ceilings of the 'Hall of Mars' at Versailles and a famous 'May' (the annually presented painting which had replaced the XVth-century Maypole) for Notre-Dame.

Bibl.: LEROY, F. N. *Histoire de Jouvenet*, Rouen and Paris, 1860. — Catalogue of *Peintres de la Réalité* Exhibition, Paris, 1934.

KALF, WILLEM.

Amsterdam ca. 1622-1693, Dutch School.

Painted *genre* scenes and still lifes in the manner of Willem Claesz Heda. He started with small works on copper representing humble kitchens and larders stacked with earthenware and pewter utensils. His second and most noteworthy period, which seems to have been influenced by Rembrandt, is that of the great still lifes, in which Chinese porcelain, precious stones, silver and golden vases and goblets are arranged on the corner of a table covered with an oriental rug. The great merit of his work lies in the ease and clarity of his composition, his mastery over his material, the depth and intensity of his colors, his fine chiaroscuro and brilliant highlights.

LASTMAN, PIETER.

Amsterdam 1583-1633, Dutch School.

Lastman was Rembrandt's master. His biblical and, less frequently, mythological scenes set in antique landscapes seem to have been influenced by Elsheimer. There is nothing idealized about the powerful forms and strong faces of his characters. Their rich colors, gorgeous garments, luxurious accessories and settings impart to his paintings an air of pomp and circumstance. The narrative effect is secured by means of gestures, sometimes reiterated.

Bibl.: FREISE, Kurt. *Pieter Lastman*. Leipzig 1911.

LA TOUR, GEORGES DE.

Lunéville 1593-1652, French School.

Brought to notice by Hermann Voss and Paul Jamot. Despite F. G. Pariset's study, La Tour's art still eludes analysis and, despite the many influences present in it, keeps its own striking originality. Recent criticism admits that he could have made the traditional journey to Rome but his name does not appear on the list of French painters in Italy. We must assume that he was influenced by Caravaggio indirectly, either through painters who had been to Rome (such as Leclerc who returned to Nancy in 1622 and could have passed on reminiscences of his master Saraceni) or, as seems more plausible, through Northern followers of Caravaggio whom he met during a visit to the Netherlands. His affinities with Honthorst and Ter Brugghen are indeed obvious; moreover his name appears among the painters of the Gallery of the Archduke Leopold William. But to these elements, he added his own peculiar poetry and graceful melancholy, and his genius was essentially original, not derivative.

Bibl.: BLOCH, V. *Georges de La Tour* in *Formes* X. 1930. Catalogue of *Peintres de la Réalité* Exhibition. Paris 1934. JAMOT, Paul. *Georges de La Tour*. Paris 1942. — ERLANGER, P. *Les Peintres de la Réalité*. 1946. — PARISET, F. G. *Georges de La Tour*. Paris 1948.

LEBRUN, CHARLES.

Paris 1619-1690, French School.

Lebrun proved his talent as a decorator when he worked with Le Sueur at the Hôtel Lambert and at Vaux (1658-1661); thereafter he was regarded as a leading spirit, indeed a dictator in the world of art. He was entrusted with the decoration of the Hall of Apollo at the Louvre and the Hall of Mirrors and that of War and Peace at Versailles. As the Director of the Gobelins Manufactory, he was responsible for the sets of tapestries dealing with *The Seasons*, *The Life of the King* and *Royal Homes*. He had much influence on contemporaries, and we may regard this as having had a detrimental effect on art, for he made it minister to the prestige of the Monarchy. He himself was a victim of the rules he enforced on his pupils, for his earliest works, the *Portrait of Jabach* (Berlin) and *Chancellor Séguier*, proved that he was capable of an honest interpretation of reality.

Bibl.: JOUIN. *Charles Lebrun et les arts sous Louis XIV*. 1889. — MARCEL, R. *Lebrun*. Paris 1909. — LEMONNIER. *L'art français au temps de Richelieu et de Mazarin*. Paris 1913.

LE CLERC, JEAN.

Nancy ca. 1590-1633, French School.

Le Clerc stayed some time in Italy, where he was the pupil and friend of Saraceni, through whom he took part in the Caravaggesque movement and was influenced by Elsheimer. Le Clerc's work is so close to Saraceni's as to be sometimes almost indistinguishable from it; the preferences for night-pieces which he brought back with him from Italy (1622) influenced his fellow-countryman La Tour. In fact, La Tour derived some of his inspiration from Le Clerc, who in turn engraved La Tour's *Veilleuses*, *Two Monks* and *The Magdalen*.

Bibl.: PARISET, F. G. *Georges de La Tour*. Paris 1948, p. 117 et seq.

LE NAIN, ANTOINE.

Laon 1588 - Paris 1648, French School.

Trained at Laon by a Dutch painter, he went to Paris in 1629 and lived with the Flemish colony. A specialist in the portrait treated as a *genre* scene. A Member of the Royal Academy of Painting from its foundation in 1648. His bold, broad technique influenced his younger brothers Louis and Mathieu to such an extent that it is sometimes difficult to distinguish between their work.

Bibl.: CHAMPFLEURY. *Les peintres de la réalité sous Louis XIII. Les Frères Le Nain*. Paris 1862. — JAMOT, P. *Les frères Le Nain*. Paris 1922. *Les Le Nain*. Paris 1929. Voss, H. Article '*Le Nain*' in *Allgemeines Kunstlexicon* (Thieme and Becker), Vol. XXIII. 1929. — FIERENS, P. *Les Le Nain*. Paris 1933. — Le Nain Exhibition. Paris 1934. (Preface by P. Jamot, Catalogue by Mlle G. Barraud.) DAVIES. *Le Nain* in *Burlington Magazine*. 1935, pp. 293-294. ISARLO, G. *Les trois Le Nain et leur suite* in *La Renaissance*, I. 1938.

LE NAIN, LOUIS.

Laon 1593 - Paris 1648, French School.

Trained by his brother Antoine, Louis Le Nain entered the Academy at the same time, but it was not long before he developed a much more individual manner. He may have stayed in Rome, and have met Velazquez who was there in 1629-1630. He was particularly interested in pictorial technique and with him we enter the realm of pure painting: he aimed at a subtle use of color, bringing out gem-like, brilliant passages against such neutral tints as greys and browns. His limpid light recalls that of Gentileschi. The works he painted in the closing years of his life are somewhat similar in feeling to those of Frans Hals. Principal works: *The Family*, *The Cart*, *Peasants at their Meal* (Louvre), *La Marquise de Forbin* (Avignon).

Bibl.: See LE NAIN, Antoine.

LE NAIN, MATHIEU.

Laon (?) 1607 - Paris 1677, French School.

Painter-in-Ordinary to the City of Paris and Member of the Royal Academy of Painting. His career was far more brilliant than those of his brothers, but his talent was more superficial and less individual. His painting is characterized by a desire to please and a touch of Mannerism. The *Corps de Garde* in the Berckheim collection is undoubtedly his best work, but, compared with similar subjects as painted by other followers of Caravaggio, it is mediocre in quality.

Bibl.: See LE NAIN, Antoine.

LE SUEUR, Eustache.

Paris 1617-1655, French School.

Le Sueur's art was influenced primarily by Vouet, who taught him, and by Raphael, whose work he knew from engravings. Although he did not make the journey to Rome, he was a classical painter by nature. His decorations for the Hôtel Lambert have been scattered, but his best work is to be found in the series of twenty-four pictures of the life of St Bruno, painted for the Carthusian Monastery in Paris. This theme suited his unadorned, delicate and lyrical style and his genuine religious feeling.

Bibl.: ROUCHES, Gabriel. *Eustache Le Sueur*. Paris 1923. JAMOT, P. *Un grand artiste chrétien en France au XVIIe: Eustache Le Sueur* in *Revue Universelle*. 1 April 1922.

LORRAIN, Claude Gellée.

Chamagne 1600 - Rome 1682, French School.

Claude Lorrain went to Italy at an early age, stayed for a while in Naples and finally settled in Rome, leaving it only from 1625 to 1627 in order to visit Venice, Bavaria and Lorraine. He studied under Agostino Tassi, from whom he learnt Elsheimer's Caravaggesque manner, but he soon became interested in effects of diffused light and turned to the landscape. It was his practice to make exact drawings from nature before starting on his paintings. He entered the lay-out of these preliminary designs in the "Libro di Verità" now in the collection of the Duke of Devonshire. His scenes from antiquity are obviously classical in conception, but when we examine the details of his canvases or study the few paintings without 'side-scenes' we realize that his landscapes are an authentic, direct interpretation of nature. He was the first painter who dared to look the sun in the face and his poetic vision, passing beyond appearances to the inner reality, had a decisive influence on Turner and the XIXth-century English landscape painters. Though we know nothing of his relations with Poussin, it appears that the latter was encouraged by his example to rediscover the true aspect of the Roman countryside. In any case, their drawings are so similar in their frank approach and response to nature that it is often hard to tell them from each other.

Bibl.: FRIEDLÄNDER. *Claude Lorrain*. Berlin 1921. — BARRÈS, Maurice. *L'art vivant*. 1926, pp. 761-765. — BOYER. *Les années d'apprentissage de Claude Lorrain à Rome* in *Actes du Congrès de l'Histoire de l'Art*. Stockholm 1933. CLARK, Kenneth. *Landscape into Art*. London 1949.

MAES, Nicolaes.

Dordrecht 1634 - Amsterdam 1693, Dutch School.

Studied under Rembrandt, but after his stay in Antwerp (1660-1665), he made a complete break with his master's style. Whereas the portraits and domestic scenes of his first period derive their chiaroscuro, their earnestness and spiritual quality from Rembrandt, after 1660 his execution became more dashing, his color-schemes grew brighter and, putting on his pigment with a more lavish brush, he secured emotional effects.

Bibl.: VALENTINER, W. *Nicolas Maes*. Stuttgart 1924.

MANFREDI, Bartolommeo.

Ostiano ca. 1580-1620, Italian School.

It is not known whether Manfredi went to Rome about 1600 or ten years later, but he adopted Caravaggio's style and imitated it so well as to give rise to a certain confusion, such as the attribution to Caravaggio of the paintings he made for the Grand Duke of Tuscany. However, his work was usually more brutal in manner and almost like a caricature of Caravaggio's. He had much influence on Nicolas Régnier and Tournier of Toulouse.

MAYNO, Fray Juan Bautista.

Madrid 1568-1649.

A native of Milan, Mayno was El Greco's pupil in Toledo in 1611 and then migrated to Madrid where he gave drawing lessons to the future King, Philip IV. His 'luminist' style is much like that of Gentileschi. He obtained remarkable effects of relief in bright tones which recall the French painters of Reality. Thus it is hardly surprising that Georges de La Tour's *Organ-Grinder* (Nantes) should have been attributed to him by L. Mayer.

METSU, Gabriel.

Leyden 1629 - Amsterdam 1667, Dutch School.

A *genre* painter in the manner of Gerard Dou and Frans Van Mieris. Like them, he depicted huntsmen, smokers, doctors, kitchen interiors and markets seen through a window. After he settled in Amsterdam (1650), his palette gained in brightness and warmth. He then took to painting conversation-pieces of small groups of people in richly decorated interiors ; the subtlety of the chiaroscuro and the harmony of the details rank his works beside those of Gerard Ter Borch. His academically treated mythological and biblical scenes and his last works with their colder range of color, their thin, smooth texture and their inexpressive faces are in the more general style of the period. He was the painter of placid bourgeois life.

MEULEN, Adam Frans van der.

Antwerp 1634 - Paris 1690, Flemish School.

Meulen studied under Pieter Saayers, a painter of historical subjects, and he too specialized in these. Summoned to Paris in 1665, he became the chronicler of Louis XIV's campaigns. He made tapestry designs for the Gobelins and had many pupils and imitators.

MICHELIN, Jean.

Langres 1623 - Jersey 1696, French School.

A member of the Academy. Owing to his Protestantism, he had to flee to Hanover in 1681. He painted 'bambocciatas' and successful pastiches of the Le Nains. His *Baker's Cart* (1656), an amusing scene of daily life, is in the Metropolitan Museum of Art, New York.

Bibl.: BLOCH, Vitale. *Autour des Le Nain* in *Beaux-Arts*. 10 August 1934. — LAZAREFF, V. *An Unknown Picture by Michelin* in *Art in America*, No. 22. Dec. 1933.

MIGNARD, Pierre.

Troyes 1612 - Paris 1695, French School.

Studied under Boucher and Bourges and worked with Vouet, before setting out for Rome (1635), where he painted Pope Urban VIII and studied the Carracci whose manner he adopted. In 1690, he succeeded Lebrun as First Painter to the King and became Chancellor of the Academy. He was a conscientious painter with a cold, conventional style. Only one of his works, the *Virgin with the Grapes* (Louvre), has any real charm ; but even this is rather stiff and affected.

Bibl.: LEBRUN-DALBANNE. *Pierre Mignard*. Paris 1878.

MOILLON, Louise.

Paris 1616-1674, French School.

Daughter of Nicolas Moillon, the landscape-painter, and sister of Isaac Moillon, the historical painter, Louise Moillon specialized in still lifes of which two charmingly graceful examples are to be found in the Musée des Augustins, Toulouse.

Bibl.: *Exposition des peintres de la Réalité*. Paris 1924.

MOMPER, Joos de.

Antwerp 1564-1635, Flemish School.

A landscape painter of the transitional period when Mannerism was gradually giving way to direct observation of nature. He painted mostly mountain landscapes and winter scenes, which have affinities with the panoramic, mountainous landscapes of the XVIth century, but show a sensitive feeling for space and light. Many of the figures in his landscapes were painted by other hands. He was very strongly influenced by Brueghel de Velours.

Bibl.: Törnell, H. G. *Joos de Momper*. 1931.

MURILLO, Bartholomé Esteban.

Seville 1618 - Cadiz 1682.

Murillo was orphaned at an early age and brought up by an aunt who left him to his own devices and let him run wild with the urchins of Seville. This was probably as good a school as any. At 24 years of age, he went to Madrid, where he was welcomed by Velazquez. He remained there for three years and then returned to Seville, where he settled down to a regular, comfortable, hard-working existence. He strove to give his religious paintings mystic overtones and to introduce supernatural elements into his scenes of family life. However, despite the sincerity of his intentions, he succeeded only in creating an artificial *genre*, in which the conventionality of the piety is conditioned by a desire to edify. His realistic scenes, which he sought to charge with human significance, convey no more than commonplace sentimentality. It is therefore hardly surprising that Murillo should have been commissioned to paint *Don Juan*. His pious portrayal of *St Elizabeth succoring the Lepers* (Madrid) and his insipid *Immaculate Conception* (Louvre) have made him a leading figure in the history of religious sentimentality, though perhaps not in the history of art.

Bibl.: Lefort, P. *Murillo et ses élèves*. Paris 1892. Monoto. *B. E. Murillo*. Seville 1923.

OSTADE, Adriaen van.

Haarlem 1610-1684, Dutch School.

A *genre* painter and a pupil of Frans Hals. He scarcely ever left Haarlem, where he found his subjects in the life of the people. He has an obvious fondness for indoor scenes of peasants drinking, dancing or fighting. His favorite subjects also include organ-grinders and the village school. The paintings of his first period, influenced by Brouwer, are predominantly grey in color and rather frigid. Later he appears to have taken over from Rembrandt a broader, more vigorous treatment. In the closing years of his life he seems to have been particularly concerned with *finish*. His brother Isaac, who studied under him, showed more originality in his winter landscapes with skaters.

Bibl.: Rosenberger, A. *Adrian und Isaac van Ostade*. Bielefeld 1900.

PACHECO, Francisco.

San Lucar de Barrameda 1564 - Seville 1654, Spanish School.

Although he never visited Italy, Pacheco was the last and best of the Spanish 'Romanists.' A distinguished and cultured man, he moved in literary circles and was an excellent theoretician. His *Arte de la Pintura* (1649) is his best work in this field. Teacher and father-in-law of Velazquez, he showed rare discrimination in recognizing his genius and encouraging him to follow his own bent. His *Embarkation of St Peter Nolasco* (Seville) is the best of a series of paintings he executed for the Monastery of the Fathers of Mercy in Seville.

Bibl.: Justi, K. *Velazquez und sein Jahrhundert*. 1923.

POST, Frans.

Leyden ca. 1612 - Haarlem 1680, Dutch School.

In 1637, Post went to Brazil with Prince Maurice of Nassau and stayed there until 1644. From memory and from sketches made on the spot, he painted Brazilian landscapes, which, besides their genuine documentary interest, are remarkably authentic in atmosphere. It was Post who introduced the exotic landscape into the Dutch School.

POTTER, Paul.

Eukhuysen 1625 - Amsterdam 1654.

A landscape and animal painter and a pupil of Lastman's. His career as a painter covers a period of only ten years, but his output was considerable. His *Bull* at The Hague (1647) demonstrates his perfect drawing and a curious combination of sophistication and naivety. Nevertheless, his painstakingly executed works are curiously lifeless; it is almost as though their painter had imbibed some of the bovine tranquillity of his subjects.

Bibl.: Michel, E. *Paul Potter*. 1907.

POUSSIN, Nicolas.

Les Andelys 1594 - Rome 1665.

Little is known about Poussin's life before 1624, except that he studied under Quentin Varin and went to Paris where he met Cavalier Marin who persuaded him to go to Rome (1624). He arrived there when the Carracci, Guido Reni and Domenichino were at the height of their fame and in this atmosphere his genius awakened. Except for a short stay in Paris in 1641-1642, he was to spend the rest of his life in Rome, shunning society, working diligently and unable to keep up with his commissions. Poussin's themes were taken from classical antiquity or the Bible and he was also interested in mythology and allegory, in which he found a medium for commentaries, whose necessity is not apparent to us, though Poussin evidently set great store on them. However, it is the painter rather than the abstruse thinker who interests us today. He was deeply sensitive to the beauty of forms and, when he dropped the thinker's mask, displayed a temperament as voluptuous as Giorgione's. His landscapes strike us as his best work; his poetic feeling for nature was so strong that his intellectual predilections were powerless to break the spell.
His principal works in chronological order are: *Death of Germanicus* (1628), *The Triumph of Flora* (1630), *Parnassus* (1635), *The Manna* (1639), *Eliezar and Rebecca* (1648), *Shepherds in Arcadia* (1653), *Orpheus and Eurydice* (1659) and *The Seasons* (1660-1664).

Bibl.: Félibien. *Entretiens sur les vies des peintres*. Trévoux 1725. — Magne, Emile. *Nicolas Poussin*. Paris 1914. Friedländer, W. *Nicolas Poussin*. Munich 1914. — Gide, André. *Poussin*. Paris 1945. — *Poussin et son temps*, Société Poussin. Paris 1947. — Jamot, P. *Nicolas Poussin*. Paris 1948.

POZZO, Andrea.

Trento 1642 - Vienna 1709, Italian School.

After teaching himself in Rome and Venice, he was taken up by the Jesuits and employed in the decoration of many of the Order's buildings, notably in Genoa, Rome, Bologna, Modena, and finally, at the request of the Emperor Leopold, in Vienna. He had amazing skill as a decorator and endowed painting with, as it were, a fourth dimension by introducing false architectural features, sumptuous illusionist realism and imaginary perspectives.

Bibl.: Voss. *Malerei des Barock in Rom*. Berlin 1924.

QUENTIN or QUANTIN, Philippe.

Dijon ca. 1600-1636, French School.

Probably visited Italy, but worked almost exclusively in

Burgundy. This *petit maitre*, who was a source of wonder and admiration to Poussin, was influenced by Caravaggio through the medium of Saraceni, but he also shows traces of Venetian influence, particularly that of Bassano. Some of his works can be seen in the Dijon and Langres Museums.

Bibl.: FYOT, E. *Le peintre Quantin*. 1914.

RÉGNIER, NICOLAS.

Maubeuge ca. 1590 - Venice 1667, French School.

Studied under Abraham Janssens in Antwerp, went to Rome (1615-1620) and frequented Caravaggesque circles, becoming acquainted with Manfredi. From 1624 to 1641, he lived in Venice and his style shows the influence of Guido Reni and the Bolognese.

Bibl.: SANDRART. *Teutsche Academie*. 1675. — Voss, H. *Anzeiger des Schlesischen Landesmuseum*. 1922, p. 47. THIEME-BECKER. *Nicolas Régnier*, Vol. XXVIII (1934), p. 90.

REMBRANDT VAN RIJN, HARMENZ.

Leyden 1606 - Amsterdam 1669, Dutch School.

Was apprenticed to Jacob Swanenburch in Leyden (1621) and then studied under Pieter Lastman in Amsterdam (1623). On his return to Leyden in 1624-1625, he commenced his career as painter with Jan Lievens. His first known works date from 1626. In 1631 he settled in Amsterdam and became a very popular portraitist until 1640. In 1634, he married Saskia van Uylenburgh and in the same year bought a magnificent house in 'Jews' Street.' In 1642, he completed the *Night Watch* and Saskia died leaving him a son, Titus, who was christened in 1641. Very probably in 1645, Hendrickje Stoffels entered his service; in 1654, she bore him a daughter, Cornelia. Between 1640 and 1648, Rembrandt's reputation was on the decline, but his genius went from strength to strength. In 1650, Rembrandt, who had acquired a large art-collection, was in grave financial straits, but his capacity for work remained unimpaired. In 1657-1660, his house and his collection were put up for public auction. Hendrickje Stoffels died in 1668 and Titus, who had just been married, died a few months later. In 1669, Rembrandt died in poverty and obscurity.

His work can be divided into three periods, each characterized by a masterpiece : youth (*The Anatomy Lesson*, 1632), maturity (*The Night Watch*, 1641) and old age (*The Syndics*, 1661).

Bibl.: MICHEL, E. *Rembrandt*. Paris 1893. — WEISBACH. *Rembrandt*. Berlin 1931. — FOCILLON, H. *Rembrandt*. Paris 1936.

RENI, GUIDO.

Calvenzano near Bologna 1575 - Bologna 1642, Italian School.

A pupil of Denis Calvaert and then of the Carracci, Guido Reni at one time hoped to surpass Caravaggio in his own field. His *Crucifixion of St Peter* at the Vatican Gallery shows him straining every effort to do this, and with much virtuosity, but he chose a smooth manner and silvery tones which often become insipid. His expressive heads, his Vatican decorations and his very fine portraits such as that of his mother made his name, but it was through his Aurora ceiling at the Casino Rospigliosi that he became the first painter in Rome, following the departure of Annibale Carracci and Caravaggio in 1609. The cupola at San Domenico in Bologna, the *Massacre of the Innocents* and then the *Assumption* for the Jesuits in Genoa, whose exhibition in Bologna had been a triumph, gave him a reputation which is not considered justified today. He refused invitations from the Kings of England and Spain, the Regent of France and the Duke of Mantua. After a journey to Naples, which he was forced to leave as a result of pressure from the Neapolitan painters, he settled in

Rome and continued painting his sickly-sweet pictures until his death.

Bibl.: MALAGUZZI, Valeri. *Guido Reni*. Florence 1921.

RIBERA, JUSEPE DE, known as LO SPAGNOLETTO.

Jativa (Valencia) 1591 - Naples 1652, Spanish School.

Studied under Ribalta and ran away to Rome at the age of sixteen. Caravaggio's art was a revelation to him. By 1626, he was living on a grand scale in Naples, a Knight of Christ and an Academician, rich and respected. He took advantage of his privileged position in Naples, which then belonged to Spain, to introduce the art of his own country, which still remained somewhat outside the main current of European painting. His direct, violent vision of life fired the enthusiasm of contemporaries, but it was limited ; his weakness is apparent in the way in which he found it necessary to stress the color, thicken the paint, emphasize lines and go over his work again and again so as to heighten the effect. He took a sadistic pleasure in painting flayed martyrs, cripples and the dregs of humanity, and the same somewhat morbid turn of mind found inverted expression in his paintings of sweet, defenceless girls, for example in his *Ecstasy of St Magdalen* and his *Conception* at Salamanca. This pietistic sentimentality is reminiscent of Murillo.

Bibl.: MAYER, A. L. *Jusepe de Ribera*. Leipzig 1923.

RIGAUD, HYACINTHE Y ROS.

Perpignan 1659 - Paris 1743, French School.

Official Portraitist to Louis XIV, Rigaud represented his reign in the way in which it aspired to be remembered, showing his models (Louis XIV, Bossuet, Frederick Augustus III and Philip V) under an idealized aspect, for the benefit of posterity. Despite the pomp and circumstance of his pictures necessitated by the punctilious etiquette of the Versailles court, he was a shrewd and, on occasion, formidable observer.

Bibl.: J. Roman edited *Le Livre de Raison*, by H. RIGAUD, in 1919.

ROSA, SALVATOR.

Renelta 1615 - Rome 1673.

Pupil of Ribera at Naples, and friend of Aniello Falcone, whose manner he imitated. Spent most of his life in Rome, but also stayed nine years with the Grand Duke of Tuscany in Florence. His reputation was made by his battle-scenes, imbued with poetic melancholy, mingling the ruins of ancient temples with tokens of the frenzy for destruction inseparable from war ; and also by his landscapes, rich in contrasts.

RUBENS, PIERRE-PAUL.

Siegen (Westphalia) 1577 - Antwerp 1640, Flemish School.

Following the death of his father, who had been living in exile, Rubens returned with his family to Antwerp and became a page in the household of the Countess de Lalaines. After an excellent education both intellectually and socially he studied under the landscape painter Verhaecht (1590), then under Van Noort (1596) and Otto Vaenius (1596-1600). He went to Italy in 1600 and entered the service of the Duke of Mantua (1600-1604). During this period, he was influenced by Veronese, Titian and Tintoretto and painted *St Helen*, the *Crowning with Thorns* and the *Elevation of the Cross* in the Hospice Civil at Grasse (1602) and the *Holy Trinity adored by members of the Gonzaga Family* (1604). In 1605, he went to Rome, where he studied Michelangelo and associated with the Bolognese painters. In 1608, he returned to Antwerp where he was appointed Court Painter to the Stadtholders and, in 1609, he married Isabel Brandt. Their wedding portrait is to be seen in the

Munich Museum. In 1611, he bought a magnificent mansion in which he placed his collection, including 19 Titians, 17 Tintorettos and 7 Veroneses. He painted the *Descent from the Cross* for Antwerp Cathedral. By 1615, he had perfected his style and his works followed one another in rapid succession : *Conversion of St Paul* (1616-1618), *The Assumption* (1620), Bacchanalia, hunting-scenes, mythological scenes giving occasion for magnificent female nudes : *The Rape of the Daughters of Leucippus* (1620), decorative paintings for the Jesuits in Antwerp, the *Story of Decius Mus* and the *Life of Marie de Medici* in twenty-one paintings for the Luxembourg Palace.

Isabel Brandt died in 1626 and in 1628 Rubens was sent on a mission to Madrid. In 1629 he was sent as Ambassador to Charles I of England, who knighted him and commissioned him to decorate the ceiling of the Palace at Whitehall. In 1630 he married Helena Fourment, who was only sixteen years of age. His works became more sentimental and developed a more subtle sensuality reminiscent of Correggio's, e.g. the *Triptych of St Ildefonso*, Vienna (1630-1632) and the *Petite Pelisse*. In 1632, Rubens was sent on a mission to the Prince of Orange and bought the Steen estate, near Malines, where he spent the closing years of his life. His works increased in brightness and subtlety and took on a lyrical intensity and warmth. His last great compositions are the *Martyrdom of St Lieven*, Brussels (1634), the *Way to Golgotha* (1637), *Landscape with Fowler* (1638) and the *Shipwreck of Aeneas* (1635).

Bibl. : PILES, R. DE. *La vie de Rubens*. Paris 1681. ROOSES, Max. *L'œuvre de P.-P. Rubens*, 5 vols. Antwerp 1886-1892. — BURCKHARDT, Jacob. *Erinnerungen aus Rubens*. Basel 1897. New Edition, Vienna 1938. — FIERENS, P. *Rubens*. 1931. — BAZIN, Germain. *P.-P. Rubens*, *L'amour de l'art*. November 1936. — Catalogue of Exhibition 'Rubens et son temps.' Paris 1936.

RUISDAEL, JACOB VAN.

Haarlem 1625 - Amsterdam 1682, Dutch School.

We know that Ruisdael belonged to a family of landscape painters, the most famous of whom was his uncle Salomon van Ruisdael, but nothing is known about his life. He was the originator of the modern conception of the landscape *motif* and was scarcely interested in anything but the sky which occupies almost the whole of his pictures. Thus he gave it height and breadth and filled it with appropriate 'architecture,' pillars and pyramides of clouds ceaselessly driven by the wind, built up in masses or ribboning the air. He had many imitators ; his best pupil was Hobbema, whose cold analytical approach failed to penetrate his master's secret.

Bibl. : VAN STECHOW. *Ruisdael*. Berlin 1938.

SAENREDAM, PIETER JANSZ.

Asserwelft 1597 - Haarlem 1665, Dutch School.

After painting portraits and landscapes in the manner of his teacher P. de Grebber, he turned to architectural painting, which he made his speciality. His paintings of churches are models of what such works should be, in their accurate observation, lighting and the angle from which they are painted. The painter seems to have approached these buildings in the same spirit as the portraitist approaches his models. The impression of space we get from his interiors is due not only to the mathematical accuracy of the perspective, but still more to the general coloring, in which greys and silvery whites prevail, giving a pleasant glow to the whole. Most of the small figures in these interiors are other painters and Adriaen Van Ostade is frequently represented.

Bibl. : SWILLENS, P. T. A. *Pieter Jansz Saenredam*. 1935.

SARACENI, CARLO.

Venice ca. 1585-1625, Italian School.

Saraceni went to Rome in the early years of the XVIIth century, and at first his procedures were much like those of Elsheimer, though with the addition of Giorgione's influence under which he had come during his early training. It is difficult to distinguish him from Jean Le Clerc, who later accompanied him to Venice and completed his decorations at the Ducal Palace after his death. His *Saint Cecilia* in the National Gallery, Rome, belongs to his best period (ca. 1620), when his style took on a new breadth and he succeeded in adapting Caravaggesque methods to his own personality.

Bibl. : PORCELLA, A. *Carlo Saraceni*, in *Rivista di Venezia*. 1928, pp. 369-412.

SEGHERS, HERCULES.

Haarlem ca. 1590 - ca. 1638, Dutch School.

His mountain landscapes and, to an even greater extent, his plains abutting on rocky cliffs mark the beginning of the true Dutch landscape. Like Rembrandt and Koninck, who were perhaps influenced by him, he had that cosmic sense which is imparted by a feeling of solitude, the infinite and the sublime. In this respect, he is a complete contrast to his contemporary Momper.

Bibl. : STEENHOFF, W. *Hercules Seghers*. Amsterdam 1924.

SNYDERS, FRANS.

Antwerp 1579-1657, Flemish School.

Studied under Pieter Brueghel the Younger (1593) and Van Balen. Went to Italy with Brueghel de Velours (1608) and specialized in still life and in the type of animal painting practiced by Oudry and Desportes in France in the following century. His pupils included Paul de Vos and Jan Fyt.

Bibl. : Catalogue of Exhibition 'Rubens et son temps,' Paris 1936.

STEEN, JAN.

Leyden 1626-1679, Dutch School.

Steen is said to have studied under Adriaen Van Ostade at Haarlem and Van Goyen at The Hague. He had a versatile talent and painted *genre* and historical pictures, mythological and biblical scenes, as well as landscapes and portraits. His early landscapes contain many figures and they recur, but in a larger form, in his best works, which are scenes from everyday life : drinking-bouts, games, brawls, etc. The world of the Dutch middle class— doctors, professional 'healers,' alchemists, women dressing —is treated with humor, but sympathetically. One of his most characteristic features was his strong sense of fun, which is displayed to the full in his paintings of children being naughty at school or during family or religious gatherings. He found scope for humor even in his renderings of biblical subjects.

Bibl. : BREDIUS, A. *Jan Steen*. Amsterdam 1927. — SCHMIDT-DEGENER and GELDER, van. *Jan Steen*. 1928.

STREECK, JURIAEN VAN.

Amsterdam 1632-1687, Dutch School.

Painted portraits and especially still lifes on the lines of those painted by Willem Kalf in his maturity. His color is at once delicate and sumptuous, his composition spare and carefully thought-out ; his properties included vases in precious metals or in Delft china, Venetian glassware, oranges and lemons arranged on a velvet tablecloth with gold fringes.

Bibl. : ZARNOWSKA, E. *La nature morte hollandaise*. Brussels 1929.

TASSEL, Richard.

Langres 1580-1660, French School.

Painter, sculptor and architect. Trained chiefly in Italy (1600-1608). He may have known Caravaggio, whose *Madonna of Loretto* he copied (Langres Cathedral). While open to modern influences, he was also interested in P. van Laar's *bambocciate*. His highly original way of seeing the world was badly served by a clumsy technique, but his portrait of an Abbess in the Dijon Museum with its striking gravity is one of the masterpieces of French portraiture and is comparable with Zubaran. Works by Tassel are to be seen in the Langres and Dijon Museums.

Bibl.: VARNEZ. *Mémoires de la Société d'Agriculture de la Haute-Marne*, vol. II.

TENIERS, David, THE YOUNGER.

Antwerp 1610 - Brussels 1690, Flemish School.

Studied under his father David Teniers the Elder. Started his career with landscapes and then, under Brouwer's influence, specialized in *genre*, historical and allegorical scenes, as from 1632. In 1937, he married Anne Brueghel, daughter of Brueghel de Velours and ward of Rubens. He had a very successful career, became Chamberlain to the Archduke Leopold William and curator of his collections. He had many pupils and his studio became a veritable picture-factory. In 1663, he founded the Academy of Brussels.

Bibl.: Monographs by PEYRE, R. Paris 1914, and Eckhoud, G. Brussels 1926.

TER BORCH, Gerard.

Zwolle 1617 - Deventer 1681, Dutch School.

Studied under Pieter Molijn at Haarlem, then went to England and to Italy, returning in 1641. He finally settled at Deventer in 1650, after a stay in the court of Philip IV of Spain. His early pictures often represented groups of soldiers and officers. Then he turned to scenes of bourgeois life: mothers and children, women reading, writing, or spinning, and the like. However, his principal work was in the portrait: the persons he depicted had an attitude befitting their rank as well as the simple properties used by the painter in order to create space around them—a chair or a table was nearly always enough. His genuine, if over-cautious, interest in such objects, which others used simply to give dimension to the space around their figures is also demonstrated in his *genre* scenes: women at their toilet, flirtations and music lessons. He excelled in the rendering of materials and avoided bright windows or openings on the outside air. His gradations of grey gave way to a richer range of color about 1670.

Bibl.: MICHEL. *Gerard Ter Burg*. Paris 1887. — HELLENS, F. G. *Ter Borch*. Brussels 1911.

TER BRUGGHEN, Hendrick.

Deventer 1588 - Utrecht 1629, Dutch School.

Studied under Abraham Bloemaert of Utrecht. From 1604 to 1614, he lived in Italy, where he was instinctively attracted towards the Saraceni and Gentileschi group and where he may have met Caravaggio. He painted scenes from the Old and, more rarely, the New Testaments, as well as a great many half-length figures midway between the *genre* painting and the portrait. No pictures can be positively attributed to him before 1620; however, the Havre *Vocation of St Matthew*, which is probably earlier, seems to be his work. The style of his pictures, which are well-lighted and painted with a full brush, probably influenced the Northern followers of Caravaggio of the 1619-1629 generation, and perhaps Georges de La Tour as well.

Bibl.: BAUMGART, F. *Beiträge zu Hendrick Ter Brugghen* in *Oud Holland*. 1929, pp. 222 et seq.

TOURNIER, Nicolas.

Montbéliard before 1600 - Toulouse (?) after 1670, French School.

Studied under Valentin and probably made the journey to Rome between 1620 and 1639. Though influenced by Caravaggio, he treated his religious subjects with a very individual dignity and feeling. His *Battle of Constantine* recalls Piero della Francesca and Aniello Falcone. His color is sustained, though dull, with purples, greens and reds placed side by side with browns. He started a school at Toulouse, which, thanks to him, became an independent art center combining the Caravaggesque and Provençal traditions. Some of his works are to be seen in the Musée des Augustins, Toulouse.

Bibl.: MESPLÉ, P. *A travers l'Art toulousain*. Toulouse 1942. — *Une école de Peinture provinciale française au XVIIe siècle, l'Ecole de Toulouse*, in *Gazette des Beaux-Arts*. March 1949. — STERLING, C. *Le Concert de Tournier de Toulouse*, in *Prométhée*. June 1939. — NAEF, Hans. *Französische Meisterwerke aus Provinzmuseen*, in *Du*. July 1951.

VALENTIN, DE BOULONGNE.

Coulommiers 1594 - Rome 1632, French School.

About 1612 Valentin set out for Rome, where he associated with the Caravaggesque group. Manfredi influenced him, but he surpassed his master and his many rivals bear witness to the fact that he was the most gifted of Caravaggio's imitators. While he borrowed the latter's themes and his striving after dramatic effect, he used them in a different spirit and liked to tell a tale; hence his fortune-tellers, scenes of military life, taverns, old soldiers and musicians. His color and his impasto are rich and solid, his tones well-defined and pungent. He gained a great reputation and Louis XIV was fond of his work.

Bibl.: SANDRART. *Teutsche Academie*. 1683, p. 368. DAUVERGNE, A. *Le Valentin, peintre né à Coulommiers-en-Brie*. 1862. — SAINT-AMOUR, C. de. *Les Boulongne*. 1919.

VELAZQUEZ, Diego da Silva y.

Seville 1599 - Madrid 1660, Spanish School.

Velazquez began his apprenticeship at an early age, studying first under Herrera el Viejo and then under Pacheco. He owed a great deal to the sympathy and culture of the latter who encouraged his realistic tendencies. He worked with Pacheco for five years and married his daughter (1618). The *Water Carrier* and *Christ in the House of Martha* were painted at this time.

Philip IV's accession and the patronage of Fonseca and then of Duke Olivarez had a decisive effect on his career and he entered the royal service in 1624. For thirty-seven years, he was to paint his master, the Infantas, the court dwarfs, etc., while at the same time carrying out increasingly exacting official duties.

His position in the court made him familiar with the Titians in the royal collections and Rubens' visit to Madrid (1628-1629), during which he shared his studio, opened up new vistas to him. Rubens urged him to visit Italy and the King gave his consent. First of all he went to Venice, then to Parma and Rome, where he was well-received by Cardinal Barberini, returning via Naples. *Vulcan's Forge* was painted in Rome during his visit. The following eighteen years saw the development of his genius, an increasing freedom of technique and an ever-greater subtlety of color. Landmarks are: the *Equestrian Portrait* of Olivarez, *Don Balthasar Carlos*, the *Surrender of Breda* (before 1635), the *Portrait of Philip IV* in the London National Gallery and *Venus and Cupid* (ca. 1642).

A second journey to Italy in 1650-1651 for the purpose of obtaining pictures for the royal collections enabled Velazquez to revisit Venice, Milan and Padua and to spend a long period in Rome where he painted the amazing *Portrait* of *Pope Innocent X*. The King recalled him and, on his return, Velazquez applied for and was granted the post of Grand Marshal of the Palace. From this time onwards, he was in charge of traveling, amusements, the furnishing of the palaces, pictures and collections. It is difficult to imagine how he was able to spare enough time from these duties to paint so many pictures, including portraits of the King and of Queen Mariana and, in particular, *Las Meninas* (1656), his spiritual testament, and the *Weavers* (1657), his artistic testament.

Bibl. : Justi, Carl. *Diego Velazquez und sein Jahrhundert.* Bonn 1888. — Mayer, A. L. *Diego Velazquez.* Berlin 1924. Dabit, E. *Les maîtres de la Peinture espagnole : Le Greco, Vélasquez.* Paris 1937. — Lafuente, E. *Velasquez.* Oxford 1943. — Fargue, L. P. *Vélasquez.* Paris 1946. — Tolnay, C. de. *Les Fileuses et les Ménines* in *Gazette des Beaux-Arts.* January 1949, pp. 21-38.

VERMEER, Jan.

Delft 1632-1675, Dutch School.

Apart from a few dates, little is known of Vermeer's life. It is known that he married in 1653 and was admitted to St Luke's Guild in the same year. Did he go to Italy, as his first works would seem to indicate, or was he in touch only with the Utrecht painters such as Ter Brugghen ? At any rate, the kinship between his *Diana and her Nymphs* and Jacob van Loo's *Diana* is undeniable. His acquaintanceship with Carel Fabritius, who was killed in the powder-mill explosion at Delft in 1654, is even less certain, but the *Procuress* (1656) in the Dresden Museum seems to echo the style of his *Young Man with a Glass,* perhaps a portrait of Vermeer. Vermeer lived at Delft, where he was much appreciated by his fellow-painters—he was twice President of St Luke's Guild—and where his works were sought after by art-lovers who paid good prices for them. In fact only Gerard Dou's works fetched as much. But his output was small and he appears to have died in poverty. He was forgotten until Thoré-Bürger rediscovered him in 1866. Since then, a little more light has been thrown on his work, although it has not been possible to date more than a few of his pictures.

Following his youthful works, which show his early influences, his personal style made itself felt in the *Woman Asleep* (Metropolitan Museum), the *Street in Delft,* the *View of Delft* and the *Milkmaid,* which seems molded in color. Thereafter, he confined himself to interiors with one figure or with very small groups. He reached full maturity about 1660, which is the date attributed to the *Portrait of a Young Girl* in the Mauritshuis at The Hague. The *Young Woman with Flute* and the *Girl in a Red Hat* (National Gallery, Washington) show greater freedom and precede the *Studio* or *Allegory of Painting,* which was painted about 1665. The *Astronomer,* the *Geographer* and the *Virginal Players* belong to his last period.

His known works do not amount to more than forty pictures and this encouraged a forger, using the early pictures as his models, to show us Vermeer in a new role, namely as a religious painter. The first of these forgeries was an excellent rendering of the *Supper at Emmaus.* However, the following works, which were less skillfully done, gave rise to suspicion and the fraud was detected.

Bibl. : Bürger, W. *Van der Meer de Delft.* Paris 1866. Vries, A. B. de. *Jan Vermeer de Delft,* followed by *La Poétique de Vermeer* by René Huyghe. Paris 1948.

VIGNON, Claude.

Tours 1593 - Paris 1670, French School.

After a short period in Lallemand's studio in Paris, Vignon went to Rome (ca. 1616) and moved in Caravaggesque circles with the pupils of Elsheimer, Poelenburg and Honthorst. He was more attracted, however, by the elegant, vivacious color texture of the Venetians. On his return to France, he was flooded with commissions for decorative work and was extremely prolific. His style is powerful, even brutal and his thick, vibrant brushwork has an impressionist quality. His kinship with Spain, which he visited on two occasions, is obvious. He influenced the young Rembrandt and took an interest in his painting.

Bibl. : Sterling, C. *Un Précurseur français de Rembrandt : Claude Vignon* in *Gazette des Beaux-Arts.* October 1934. Besnard, C. *Claude Vignon* (Thesis for Louvre School).

VOUET, Simon.

Paris 1590-1649, French School.

Precociously gifted as a youth, Vouet traveled to England, Constantinople and Venice, stayed in Rome from 1614-1621 and then in Genoa and Venice. By 1624, his fame had become so great that he was elected Prince of St Luke's Academy, Rome. On returning to France in 1627, he dropped his 'dark' manner and took up decorative work. His success lasted until the advent of Poussin in 1641. He was kept in the background by Lebrun and was not elected to the Academy of Painting when it was founded. Not long afterwards, he died in obscurity. He had a real feeling for art, but his superficial talent was capable only of absorbing the styles of the various Italian masters and was essentially uncreative. He taught François Perrier, Dufresnoy, Pierre Mignard, Le Sueur and Lebrun, but his pupils soon broke away from him retaining only certain technical procedures he had taught them.

Bibl. : Demonts, L. *Simon Vouet* in *Bulletin de la Société Histoire de l'Art français.* 1913. — Voss, Hermann, in *Zeitschrift für bildende Kunst.* 1924, pp. 56-57. — Dimier, L. *Histoire de la Peinture française. Du retour de Vouet à la Mort de Lebrun.* Paris 1926.

WITTE, Emmanuel de.

Alkmaar 1617 - Amsterdam 1692, Dutch School.

De Witte specialized mainly in interiors, particularly church interiors, in which carefully planned perspective, powerful natural lighting and the choice of color—yellowish white in the bright parts and greyish white in the shadows—gave an impressive vastness, to which the figures, few and far between, contributed. Other works of his that have come down to us are seascapes, landscapes with figures, mythological scenes and *genre* paintings, particularly market scenes.

Bibl. : Bode. *Die Meister der Holländischen und Flämischen Malerschulen.* Leipzig 1919, p. 271.

ZURBARAN, Francisco.

Fuente de Cantos 1598 - Madrid 1664, Spanish School.

A simple, upright, pious man, whose life was uneventful. All his work was done for convents and churches ; thus he is the painter *par excellence* of Catholic, mystic-minded Spain of the XVIIth century. The supernatural for him was the truest reality and, by dint of scrupulous objectivity, he succeeded in penetrating beyond the mask of physical appearance to the inmost soul of things.

In 1638-1639, when he had gained full mastery of his inspiration and his technique, he finished his paintings for the Carthusian Monastery in Jenez and the Monastery in Guadeloupe. His later works, those painted after 1645, are devotional paintings, mostly for South America, and reflect both the haste in which they had to be painted and the less refined taste of his new *clientèle.*

Bibl. : Cascales y Munoz, J. *F. de Zurbaran. Su epoca, su vida y su obras.* Madrid 1911. — Kehrer, H. *F. de Zurbaran.* Leipzig 1918. — Gaya Nuno, J. A. *Zurbaran.* Barcelona 1948.

FRANCE

CHAMPFLEURY. *Les Peintres de la Réalité sous Louis XIII.* Paris 1862.

FONTAINE, A. *Les Doctrines d'Art en France de Poussin à Diderot.* Paris 1909.

Catalogue of the Exhibition *Paysage français de Poussin à Diderot.* Paris 1909.

DIMIER, L. *Histoire de la Peinture française : Du retour de Vouet à la mort de Lebrun, 1627-1650.* Paris-Brussels 1926-1927.

WEISBACH, W. *Französische Malerei des XVII. Jahrhunderts.* Berlin 1932.

Catalogue of the Exhibition *Peintres de la Réalité.* Paris 1934.

ERLANGER, Ph. *Les Peintres de la Réalité.* Paris 1946.

SPAIN

PACHECO, F. *Arte de la Pintura.* Seville 1649.

MAYER, A. L. *Historia de la Pintura Española.* Madrid 1928.

LAFUENTE, E. *El realismo en la Pintura del Siglo XVII en Espana.* Barcelona 1935.

SERULLAZ. *Evolution de la Peinture espagnole.* Paris 1947.

GUINARD, P. and BATICLE, J. *Histoire de la Peinture espagnole.* Paris 1950.

FLANDERS AND THE LOW COUNTRIES

FROMENTIN. *Les Maîtres d'autrefois.* Paris 1876.

BERTOLOTTI. *Giunte agli artisti belgi ed olandesi in Roma nei sec. XVI-XVII.* Rome 1885.

BODE, W. von. *Die Meister der Holländischen und Vlämischen Malerschulen.* Leipzig 1917.

FRIEDLÄNDER. *Die Niederländischen Maler des XVII. Jahrhunderts.* Berlin 1923.

GROSSE, R. *Die Holländische Landschaftskunst, 1606-1650.* Berlin 1925.

MUCHALL-VIEBROOK. *Flemish Drawings of the XVIIth Century.* London 1926.

BRIÈRE-MISME. *La Peinture hollandaise.* Paris 1927.

CLAUDEL, P. *Introduction à la Peinture hollandaise.* Paris 1935.

Catalogue of the Exhibition *Rubens et son temps.* Paris 1936.

BERNT, W. *Die Niederländischen Maler des XVII. Jahrhunderts.* Munich 1948.

BAZIN, G. *Les grands maîtres hollandais.* Paris 1950.

Catalogue of the Exhibition *Flaminghi e Italia.* Bruges 1951.

GENERAL

FÉLIBIEN. *Entretiens sur les œuvres des plus excellents peintres.* Paris 1666.

SANDRART. *Teutsche Academie.* Nuremberg 1675.

HAUSENSTEIN, W. *Der Geist des Barocks.* Munich 1921.

MICHEL, A. *Histoire de l'art,* vol. VI, 1st Part : *L'art en Europe au XVII* siècle. Paris 1921.

WEISBACH, W. *Der Barock als Kunst des Gegenreformation.* Berlin 1921.

MALE, E. *L'art religieux après le Concile de Trente.* Paris 1932.

SCHNURER, G. *Katholische Kirche und Kultur in der Barockzeit.* Paderborn 1937.

REY, R. *L'art en Europe au XVII* siècle in *Histoire générale de l'art.* Paris 1938.

ISARLO, G. *Caravage et le Caravagisme européen,* vol. II, Catalogues. Aix-en-Provence 1941.

COLOMBIER, P. du. *Histoire de l'art.* Paris 1942.

LAVEDAN, P. *Histoire de l'art : Moyen âge et Temps modernes.* Paris 1944.

PIRENNE, J. *Les grands courants de l'Histoire universelle.* Paris 1946.

BERL, E. *Histoire de l'Europe,* vol. II. Paris 1947.

CLARK, K. *Landscape into Art.* London 1949.

MUMFORD, L. *Technique et Civilisation.* Paris 1950.

ITALY

BELLORI. *La Vita de pittori, scultori et architetti moderni.* Rome 1672.

VOSS, H. *Die Malerei der Spätrenaissance in Rom und Florenz.* Berlin 1920.

VOSS, H. *Malerei des Barocks in Rom.* Berlin 1925.

MOSCHINI, V. *La pittura italiana del Settecento.* Florence 1931.

MARANGONI, M. *Arte barocca : revisioni critiche.* Florence 1933.

Catalogue of the Caravaggio Exhibition. Milan 1951.

GENERAL INDEX

COLORPLATES

PRINTED IN SWITZERLAND

THIS VOLUME OF THE COLLECTION

THE GREAT CENTURIES OF PAINTING

WAS PRINTED BY THE IMPRIMERIE LA CONCORDE, LAUSANNE

FINISHED THE TENTH DAY OF OCTOBER

NINETEEN HUNDRED AND FIFTY-ONE